This Book Belongs To

THE BOOK OF
Queens

**Legendary LEADERS,
Fierce FEMALES, and
WONDER WOMEN
Who Ruled THE WORLD**

**STEPHANIE
WARREN DRIMMER**

NATIONAL GEOGRAPHIC
WASHINGTON, D.C.

Contents

Maria Theresa of Austria,
Queen of the Golden Age

Diane von Fürstenberg,
Queen of Fashion

Maya Lin, Monarch of Monuments

Eugenie Clark,
Sovereign of Sharks

Diana, Princess of Wales:
Princess With a Purpose

All Hail the Queen!

Joan of Arc, the girl who started a war

Simone Biles,
Queen of
the Beam

You might think life as a monarch sounds pretty sweet. After all, there are the royal jewels to wear, frequent feasts in your honor, and a swarm of subjects ready to carry out your every command. But being in charge isn't always all it's cracked up to be. What does it mean to be a queen?

It Isn't Easy Being Queen

Many of the queens in these pages were women fighting for power in a man's world. They took charge when their husbands died, or ruled in place of sons too young to take the throne. Their subjects were often skeptical—or downright angry—at the prospect of having a woman in charge. These queens had to prove their might at every turn. Again and again, throughout history, they showed they had the grit and guts, the smarts and skill, and the confidence and commitment to lead.

Not all of history's queens were successful. Like their male counterparts, many lost wars, empires, and the trust of their subjects. Some gave up the throne in disgrace—and a few were so hated by their subjects that their reigns came to an end when the people cried, "Off with her head!"

But many queens were up to the challenge. They led powerful nations into some of their most successful eras. From mighty monarchs who strapped on armor to defend their kingdoms to modern leaders setting a new course for the future, they proved that women can rule just as well as men.

Queens of Their Field

Queens who wore crowns and wielded scepters aren't the only kind worth honoring. In *The Book of Queens* you'll find modern (nonroyal) leaders like presidents and prime ministers and also meet women who haven't ruled nations at all: Instead, they've led people, headed movements, or guided progress. CEOs, scientists, and pioneers; artists, athletes, musicians, and writers—they may never have sat upon a gilded throne, but all are leading ladies who've made a mark on the world.

Some of the stories in these pages might be familiar. But many others might leave you wondering why so many brave, smart, and hardworking women have gone unnoticed ... until now.

As you read *The Book of Queens*, keep an eye out for these royal extras:

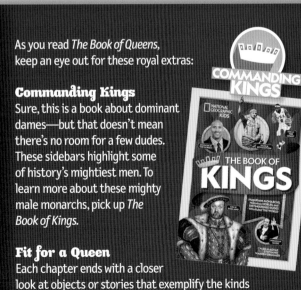

Commanding Kings
Sure, this is a book about dominant dames—but that doesn't mean there's no room for a few dudes. These sidebars highlight some of history's mightiest men. To learn more about these mighty male monarchs, pick up *The Book of Kings*.

Fit for a Queen
Each chapter ends with a closer look at objects or stories that exemplify the kinds of queens you've just learned about.

Chapter One

EMPIRE
BUILDERS

Leading nations isn't for the faint of heart: To earn a place among the greatest rulers in history, the women in this chapter had to lay everything on the line for their kingdoms. Some used smarts, skill, and shrewd negotiating to keep their nations safe. Others were ruthless rulers who expanded their lands by conquering new territories and everyone in them. Whether they were queens, empresses, presidents, or prime ministers, all reigned tirelessly to build and defend their empires. While they were at it, they left lasting marks on history.

Corazon Aquino,
first woman
elected president
of the Philippines

Himiko

❧ First Ruler of Japan ❧

When Empress Himiko, sometimes called Pimiko, came to power, Japan was not the single country it is today. It was made up of hundreds of individual nations scattered across the area's archipelago. It would take a powerful ruler to control not just one of these nations but to unify them all into an empire. Himiko rose to the challenge and became the first ruler of the new kingdom—and the first known ruler in Japanese history.

SORCERESS QUEEN

At the end of the second century, Japan was in turmoil. Without one ruler to bring together its hundreds of nations, the islands were rocked by constant conflict. The people needed a leader. So they came together and agreed on one: Himiko. It's tough to separate legend from truth in the ancient tales about her. Some say she was a shamaness, or priestess, renowned throughout Japan for her powers of sorcery. The people believed this magical monarch could speak to the gods on their behalf. According to the stories, Himiko went to live in a fortress guarded by 100 men, with 1,000 female attendants on hand to answer her every wish. Himiko focused on communicating with the divine; she never appeared in public, and her brother acted as her spokesperson to relay her words to her subjects. And she pushed her power beyond Japan's borders: Himiko sent diplomats at least four times to the neighboring nation of China. Though there's little documentation

Some historians now think that Himiko was one of several priestess queens who ruled early Japan.

Royal Rundown

❀ **BORN:** ca 3rd century A.D., Japan ❀ **DIED:** ca A.D. 248, Japan ❀ **LED:** The pre-Japanese federation of Yamatai ❀ **REMEMBERED FOR:** Becoming the first known ruler of Japan

of Himiko's reign, those missions must have been a success: The Chinese sent her 100 ceremonial bronze mirrors—a symbol of great wealth and status at the time.

BURIED MYSTERY

After turning a ragtag band of nations into an empire, Himiko managed to maintain peace and order until her death in about the year 248. Historical texts say that, to honor their departed queen, her people built a massive burial mound. It was probably one of the first *kofun*, or tombs, ever built. These large earthen mounds, shaped like keyholes, dot the landscape of Japan and hold the remains of deceased rulers.

In 2009, a team of Japanese archaeologists investigated a kofun in Sakurai City, in Nara. At 919 feet (280 m) long, it is much larger than other burial mounds in the region. The team used radiocarbon dating to find out the age of artifacts discovered near the site, dating them to between A.D. 240 and 260—the very time when Himiko died. That evidence led the scholars to believe it was the final resting place of the fabled queen. Others disagree, but no one can know for sure without excavating the tomb—something the current emperor, himself a descendant of Himiko, has forbidden.

SYMBOL OF POWER

As the centuries went by and Japan was ruled by generations of male-only emperors, Himiko became lost to history. But historians rediscovered the great shamaness-queen, and today Himiko is a celebrated figure in her homeland. She's commemorated in statues, revered in an annual bonfire festival, and has inspired characters in films, novels, and anime. Himiko has even become a symbol of a new movement to allow women to inherit the throne and become emperor of Japan—a return to the days when the nation was ruled by a powerful and beloved queen.

This mirror (above) is said to have belonged to Himiko.

Japan's Great Defender

COMMANDING KINGS

Hojo Tokimune (1251–1284)

As a nation made up of islands, Japan is a difficult place to take over; for much of history, it proved too tough for foreign invaders. But that almost changed in the 13th century, when the great warrior Kublai Khan—who had already conquered China, Mongolia, and much of the known world—set Japan as his next target. But Japan's ruler, Hojo Tokimune, refused to pay tribute: If Kublai Khan wanted Japan, his horses had better learn to swim. In the meantime, Tokimune ordered the construction of state-of-the-art defenses along western Japan, complete with seawalls to make landing ships difficult. In 1281, Kublai Khan put the system to the test and sent a huge army—nearly 140,000 soldiers—straight at Japan. But the defenses held, aided by a timely typhoon that destroyed the invading fleet. His warrior work done, Tokimune devoted the rest of his life to Zen Buddhism.

COMMANDING WOMEN

∽ Queens of the Golden Age ∽

During the centuries when these women ruled, almost all monarchs were men. These queens and empresses had to use every ounce of savvy and sovereignty they had to keep and hold the throne. They weren't always kind and just, but they were powerful rulers who made their countries into mighty kingdoms.

Power at All Costs:
Catherine the Great (1729–1796)

Brilliant and ambitious, Catherine II, known as Catherine the Great, stopped at nothing to build Russia into a world power. When she took the throne in 1762 as empress, Russia had a reputation as a place stuck in the past. Catherine worked to change this image, expanding education and the arts. She reorganized the Russian government and grew her country's territory, taking control of Crimea (a peninsula in eastern Europe) and parts of Poland. Though she began her reign intending to free the forced farm laborers called serfs (common in medieval Europe), in the end she actually strengthened the system that kept them oppressed. And her territory conquests often came at the expense of her people, who suffered under the hardships of war. But under her rule, Russia became an empire strong enough to earn a place in the ranks of Europe's most powerful countries.

Peace and Prosperity:
Queen Elizabeth I (1533–1603)

Young Elizabeth had a lot on her plate when she became queen of England in 1558. Her armies were fighting with France, and her people were fighting each other as the Roman Catholic and Protestant faiths clashed. Elizabeth ended the war with France, put a stop to religious fighting, and instituted a period of peace that lasted through her 44-year reign—the longest in her country's history to that point. Elizabeth supported theater (especially writer William Shakespeare), sent explorers such as Sir Francis Drake across the globe, and defeated the Spanish fleet when it tried to take control of England. The Elizabethan age is remembered today for its peace and prosperity.

A New Age:
Queen Victoria (1819–1901)

When the crown was placed on 18-year-old Victoria's head in 1837, her first request as ruler was to have an hour alone—something the monarch, who had been raised in a palace under strict supervision—had never experienced. Though she was only 4 feet 11 inches (1.5 m) tall, what Queen Victoria lacked in stature she made up in might. During her 63-year reign, her country experienced one of its most successful periods in history, called the Victorian age. Her rule saw the development of new technology, like the telegraph, a rail system that spread throughout Great Britain, and new scientific achievements, such as Charles Darwin's theory of evolution.

Victoria took control of vast territories, including Canada, Australia, India, and parts of Africa and the South Pacific, expanding Great Britain into an empire. By strategically arranging the marriages of her nine children into royal houses all over the world, Victoria also influenced foreign politics. And after all that, she still made time for the most famous love story of the 19th century: In 1839, Victoria fell in love with German royal prince Albert. As the head of state, she proposed to him, and then wore a white dress when they wed—setting a trend for brides that endures today.

Controversy and Controls:
Maria Theresa (1717–1780)

One of the most powerful rulers of her time, archduchess of Austria, queen of Hungary and Bohemia, and Holy Roman empress Maria Theresa ruled with an iron fist. Her father, Charles VI, had no sons to take over the throne, so he decreed that Maria Theresa, his eldest daughter, had the right to rule. But he left behind a nation that was bankrupt and almost without an army. Maria Theresa had been trained only in the "womanly" arts of painting, drawing, dancing, and music. She wasn't prepared for the challenge of turning her country around—but she did it anyway.

She increased the size of the army, beautified the capital city of Vienna, reformed the justice system by establishing a high court, and set up a new schooling system meant to bring education to all. In her free time, she had 16 children—one of whom was Marie Antoinette (p. 60). But she used her power for bad as well as good: Famously intolerant, Maria Theresa persecuted Protestants, Jews, and those she saw as "immoral." A deeply flawed ruler, Maria Theresa unified her monarchy and changed her country forever.

Empress Cixi

∾ From Powerless to Powerful ∾

Empress Cixi launched China's first rail line.

Empress Cixi started out as an ordinary girl. At 16, she was chosen by the emperor of China to be one of the many nameless women of his court. Less than 10 years later, she had become the ruler of one-third of the world's population.

Cixi rose to power on sheer cleverness. When she and the emperor had a son together, Cixi saw an opportunity. The child was the only male heir, so he inherited the throne when the emperor died in 1861. But because the child was only five years old at the time, the emperor had selected a board of advisers to rule in his stead. Along with a co-regent, Cixi overthrew the advisers, imprisoning five of them and sending the other three to their deaths. She took power for herself, and she didn't let it go for nearly the next five decades.

Even though the customs of court dictated that women were to be kept inferior to men, Cixi managed to find a way around every rule designed to hold her back: Unable to speak directly to her ministers, she led meetings from behind a screen. When her gender prevented her from taking action herself, the loyal men she kept by her side carried out her bidding. And she used a network of spies to keep tabs on everything that was happening in her kingdom.

Cixi was set on modernizing China, but her plan was unpopular with many. Change was slow, but eventually Cixi's persistence got her what she wanted. She instituted a series of reforms that banned the tradition of foot binding (wrapping the feet of young girls tightly to change the shape of their feet) and decreed a free press and democratic elections. The empress was famous for using whatever means necessary to get what she wanted: Before she died, in 1908, many believe her final act was poisoning China's next rightful ruler to make sure her own great-nephew would take the throne.

Royal Rundown

BORN: November 29, 1835, Beijing, China **DIED:** November 15, 1908, Beijing, China
LED: China **REMEMBERED FOR:** Modernization of China

Eleanor of Aquitaine

∾ Queen in a King's World ∾

History books sometimes cast Eleanor as second fiddle to her famous husbands and sons. But this queen was not only a ruler in her own right; she was one of the most powerful people in 12th-century Europe.

When Eleanor was 15, her father, the Duke of Aquitaine, died, leaving her his title and a vast stretch of lands. Suddenly, Eleanor was the most sought-after single woman in Europe. Three months later, she married King Louis VII and became the queen of France.

Eleanor was quick-witted and intelligent—qualities her husband did not share. Tensions rose between the pair, and they divorced in 1152. But Eleanor didn't waste any time coming back to power: Two months later, she was married to Henry of Anjou, and they became king and queen of England two years later, when Henry inherited the throne. In her new position, Eleanor turned the court into a center for poetry and the arts.

In 1173, two of Eleanor's sons with Henry revolted against their father to seize the throne—and it is rumored that Eleanor was behind the plot to secure the crown for her children. She was arrested and imprisoned for the next 16 years. When she was released, she was in her late 60s (considered ancient for the time), but she jumped right back into ruling, acting as the stand-in monarch when the new king, her eldest son, Richard I—also known as Richard the Lionheart—went to join the Crusades. When Richard died without an heir, Eleanor feared her dynasty would collapse. Though she was nearly 80 years old, she crossed the Pyrenees mountains to fetch her granddaughter, Blanche of Castile, so she could marry her into the French monarchy. Eleanor continued to wield her influence until her death, in 1204.

Though not all scholars agree it's true, legend says that Eleanor is famous for beginning a "Court of Love" that made poems, songs, and books about romance fashionable.

Royal Rundown

✿ **BORN:** ca 1122, Poitiers, France ✿ **DIED:** 1204, Poitiers, France ✿ **LED:** England and France
✿ **REMEMBERED FOR:** Becoming queen of England and France and one of the most powerful people in medieval Europe

REBEL, REBEL

❧ *Queens Who Fought Back* ❧

These rulers were forces to be reckoned with. When foreign invaders threatened their people, these daring dames didn't fold. Instead, they went on the offensive: raising armies, increasing their power, and mounting rebellions. Not all succeeded, but all went down in history.

Fierce Fighter:
Rani Lakshmi Bai (ca 1835–1858)

Many call Rani Lakshmi Bai "India's Joan of Arc" (p. 44). Her mother died when she was a young child, leaving her father to raise her. He trained his daughter in the art of war: riding elephants, sword fighting, and shooting a crossbow. At 14, Lakshmi Bai married the maharaja, or king. When the British later tried to take over her kingdom, the young rani, or queen, refused. She called her people to revolt against foreign rule— and commanded her rebel army herself. In 1858, British forces surrounded the rebel stronghold in overwhelming numbers. But even in the face of certain defeat, Lakshmi Bai did not surrender. She made her escape with a small force of palace guards. A few months later, she regrouped the rebels, which included women fighters. Dressed in full warrior regalia, with her army behind her, she mounted one last heroic attack— and died a martyr, fighting for her country.

Freer of Slaves:
Nanny of the Maroons (ca 1680s–ca 1730s)

There is little written evidence about her life, but stories of "Queen Nanny" have been passed down from generation to generation of Jamaican people. Nanny was born in Ghana, Africa, and brought to Jamaica as a slave. There, she was sold to a sugarcane plantation, where she labored under terrible conditions until she could bear slavery no longer. Nanny ran away from the plantation and joined the Maroons, runaway slaves living in hiding. As she grew up among them, Nanny worked to unite the Maroon communities. From her base, called Nanny Town, she organized the people to raid plantations for weapons and food, burn down plantations, and help freed slaves back to Nanny Town. During her rule, Nanny freed more than 1,000 slaves. She was revered as Queen Nanny and is, to this day, the only female national hero of Jamaica.

Independence Fighter: Yaa Asantewaa (ca 1840–1921)

Yaa Asantewaa was born into one of the wealthiest and most powerful kingdoms in 19th-century Africa, the Ashanti Confederacy (now part of modern-day Ghana). But when Asantewaa came to power in the 1880s, her nation's power was shaken. Civil wars had torn apart her people, the capital had been burned down, and British troops had set up a fort across from her palace. After her brother, the *ejisuhene*, or king, died, it fell to Asantewaa to choose the next ruler. She nominated her grandson, but the British sent him out of the country in exile. Then the invaders went too far—they demanded the Golden Stool, the throne of the Ashanti Confederacy and the beloved symbol of its power. Asantewaa had had enough. She called upon her people to fight. She strode onto the battlefield, lofting her weapon high, at the head of an army in the War of the Golden Stool. Though she was captured by enemy troops, she sparked a movement for independence and has inspired generations of young girls in Ghana.

Savior of the People: Anna Nzinga (ca 1583–1663)

At the turn of the 17th century, the independent nations of central Africa found their way of life in danger. Portugal threatened to take over the region to control the trade of African slaves throughout the world. But one African ruler had the smarts and power to stand up against the invasion: Queen Anna Nzinga. In 1626, the queen fled west with her people, beyond the reach of the Portuguese, where she founded a new state called Matamba (today, it's a region in Angola). There, Nzinga trained her people as soldiers and offered sanctuary to runaway slaves to boost her numbers. Then she shrewdly established her new kingdom as a trading gateway to the African interior. Portugal was forced to recognize Nzinga's power and deal with her as an equal. Queen Anna Nzinga was able to maintain her kingdom's independence from Portugal until her death in 1663.

Liliuokalani

⤳ The Last Queen of Hawaii ⤶

People today know Hawaii as one of America's 50 states, but not too long ago, Hawaii was its own independent nation, ruled by monarchs. One of these was Liliuokalani. The first—and last—queen of Hawaii, she spent her reign trying to keep her country independent. Though she ultimately failed, her legend lives: The story of a ruler who put her kingdom before herself.

> "Never cease to act because you fear you may fail."
> —*Liliuokalani*

LOST KINGDOM

With its white sand beaches, serene sunsets, and palm trees waving gently in the warm ocean breeze, Hawaii is a true paradise—one that nations have wanted to control for thousands of years.

Royal Rundown

❀ **BORN:** September 2, 1838, Honolulu, Hawaii ❀ **DIED:** November 11, 1917, Honolulu, Hawaii ❀ **LED:** Hawaii
❀ **REMEMBERED FOR:** Making a last stand to save her nation

According to Hawaiian legends, the islands were settled by several waves of immigrants from multiple islands in ancient Polynesia. Skilled in hunting, fishing, and farming, the Hawaiians grew into a sophisticated society ruled by chiefs and priests.

In 1778, British captain James Cook arrived on the islands, setting off four decades of conflict between Hawaiians and Westerners. Diseases like cholera and tuberculosis decimated the Hawaiian population, which fell from more than 600,000 to fewer than 24,000 in little more than a century.

Hawaii's position in the Pacific Ocean makes it the ideal location for an island military base. Nations like Great Britain, Japan, Germany—and especially the nearby United States—began to jockey for control of it. Starting in 1820, colonists from the United States moved to the island nation and took control of its sugar plantations and trade. In 1893, the United States overthrew the Hawaiian monarchy, and Hawaii became a U.S. territory.

FIGHT FOR FREEDOM

As outsiders gained control of their land and economy, there was little Hawaii could do to fight back. But one person was determined to try: Lîliuokalani, who inherited the kingdom from her brother, Kalākaua, in 1891. Four years before, he had been forced by armed soldiers to sign a new constitution that stripped the Hawaiian monarchy of its power. Lîliuokalani saw this for what it was: the first step toward the United States overthrowing the kingdom and taking over the islands. As soon as she assumed the throne, she began working to reverse the unfair constitution forced on her people and to write a new one. But the powers that now controlled her nation wanted to stop her. On January 16, 1893, United States troops landed on her shore. Unable to stand up to the United States' superior military and unwilling to shed the blood of her people, Lîliuokalani had no choice but to give up command of her nation.

But she didn't give up the fight. Hawaii's temporary government, made up of European and American business holders, refused to recognize her as rightful ruler.

A life-size statue of Lîliuokalani stands in downtown Honolulu, Hawaii. The six-foot (1.8-m) likeness is often decorated with leis and flowers by passersby.

Thousands of Hawaiians signed petitions of protest, and Lîliuokalani herself traveled to Washington, D.C., to make her case. But Hawaii was annexed as a U.S. territory anyway. Lîliuokalani was finally silenced when she was arrested and imprisoned on January 16, 1895, for conspiring in an attempted counterrevolution—though she insisted she knew nothing about it. In 1895, she was forced to formally abdicate the throne so that supporters of hers who had been jailed would be released. Lîliuokalani was pardoned and set free in 1896, but the Kingdom of Hawaii was gone forever.

ICON OF THE PEOPLE

Though Lîliuokalani's attempts to win back her country failed, she was beloved by the Hawaiian people. An accomplished musician, Lîliuokalani used her time as a prisoner to compose many songs, including one called "Aloha 'Oe," or "Farewell to Thee," now one of Hawaii's most famous anthems. She lived out the end of her life as a private citizen and died at her home in Honolulu in 1917. Today, the last queen of Hawaii is celebrated as a symbol of Hawaiian culture and independence.

Corazon Aquino

∾ The "People Power" President ∾

Often pictured in her trademark yellow dress, Corazon Aquino was a symbol of hope to her nation during its difficult transition to democracy. Aquino started out in the background of politics in the Philippines, raising her five children as her politician husband campaigned. But when he was assassinated by dictator Ferdinand Marcos in 1983, Aquino couldn't stay quiet.

In 1986, Aquino ran for office against Marcos. When he reported that he had won, she and her supporters challenged the outcome, claiming that he had falsified election results. That's when the tide began to turn: Government officials declared their support for Aquino, and Marcos fled the country. Aquino became the first female president of the Philippines—and the first female president in all of Asia. She was named *Time* magazine's Woman of the Year for 1986.

Aquino's critics said she was too passive and too inexperienced to deal with her country's severe problems, such as widespread poverty, warfare, and political corruption. And during a 1985 interview, Aquino herself famously said, "What on earth do I know about being president?" But for many Filipino people, her political prowess wasn't the point: Aquino embodied the belief their country could become a better place. She held to what she believed and retained control of her government even as powerful opponents tried to take it away. She kept the presidency for six tumultuous years, until her former defense secretary peacefully succeeded her in 1992. When Aquino died in 2009, her people mourned her passing. They tied yellow ribbons around their heads and on trees in their neighborhoods to show their respect for a woman who had worked tirelessly to bring freedom to their nation.

"I would rather die a meaningful death than live a meaningless life."
—*Corazon Aquino*

Royal Rundown

❀ **BORN:** January 25, 1933, Paniqui, Tarlac, Philippines ❀ **DIED:** August 1, 2009, Makati, Philippines
❀ **LED:** The Philippines ❀ **REMEMBERED FOR:** Guiding the Philippines during its transition to a democracy

Violeta Barrios de Chamorro

❧ The Unlikely Revolutionary ❧

Born to a wealthy ranching family, Violeta Barrios spent a sheltered childhood riding horses in the Nicaraguan countryside. But her world was rocked when her country was torn apart by civil war and the dictator Anastasio Somoza rose to power in 1936.

In 1950, she married Pedro Chamorro, a journalist for *La Prensa*, an opposition newspaper that spoke out against Somoza. The newspaper called for a revolution, with Chamorro at its head. But the movement experienced a big setback when the dictator murdered Chamorro in 1978 to silence him. Violeta Chamorro knew what she had to do. She took the reins of *La Prensa* herself, helping to lead the revolution to return her country to democracy. By 1988, she was the most outspoken voice against the dictatorship. When it was announced that free elections would be allowed in 1990, Chamorro decided to run. Even though she had a broken kneecap from a fall, she campaigned tirelessly to sweep the opposition and take her seat as Nicaragua's democratic president. She was the first woman in Central America to ever hold the title.

Chamorro's problems, however, were just beginning. There was raging inflation, debt, and unemployment to deal with. But she held her head high and focused on improving the economy and uniting her people after years of civil war. She also created protected areas of land that her people still enjoy today. In 1997, when her term ended and she handed over the presidency, her country was more peaceful and unified than it had been in years.

Royal Rundown

🌼 **BORN:** October 18, 1929, Rivas, Nicaragua 🌼 **LED:** Nicaragua 🌼 **KNOWN FOR:** Leading a revolution and Nicaragua's transition to a democratic government

"Reconciliation is much more beautiful than victory."
—*Violeta Barrios de Chamorro*

PIONEERING
POLITICIANS

The modern world didn't elect its first female leader until 1960. Since then, more and more women have fought their way to the top. Some had roles that were mostly ceremonial, but others were a defining part of their country's history.

The People's Prime Minister:
Indira Gandhi (1917–1984)

Indira Gandhi had been a revolutionary since childhood. Her father, Jawaharlal Nehru, was a leading figure in India's battle for independence from British rule, and Indira followed in her father's footsteps. After watching rebels throw British-made products into a bonfire in protest, Gandhi—at just five years old—burned her beloved doll because the toy had been made in England.

In 1966, Gandhi became India's prime minister—the first and, to date, the only woman to hold the post. Gandhi had earned the support of the people when she began her Green Revolution—agricultural reforms that helped lessen the country's food-shortage problem. But her rule was fraught with controversy, too: After serving three terms as prime minister, she was voted out of office in 1977—and briefly jailed—for instituting strict policies that took away her people's constitutional rights. Three years later, she was reelected, serving until her assassination in 1984.

Human Rights Defender
Michelle Bachelet (1951–)

Michelle Bachelet is Chile's first ever female president. First elected in 2006 and then reelected in 2014, Bachelet is known for her human rights advocacy. But the path to the presidency wasn't easy. In 1973 a brutal military takeover occurred in her country, resulting in the death and imprisonment of many people, including her own family. Bachelet herself was captured and tortured. Eventually she was able to flee the country but was forced to live in exile. Bachelet finally returned to Chile in 1979 and entered politics, in particular speaking out for children traumatized by political violence. Between her first and second terms, she became executive director of United Nations Women, a division of the UN that promotes gender equality. Today, she is the High Commissioner of Human Rights for the UN.

A Legacy of Helping Women:
Benazir Bhutto (1953–2007)

The first female leader of a Muslim nation in modern history, Benazir Bhutto had a tumultuous political career that ended with her assassination in 2007. Bhutto became the head of her father's party, the Pakistan People's Party, after he was executed when military dictator Mohammed Zia-ul-Haq took power in 1979. When Zia died in a plane crash in 1988, Bhutto won the election and became the new prime minister. She inherited a country battling poverty, crime, racial tension, and corruption in the government. But she managed to make strides, including establishing the Benazir Income Support Program, which to this day distributes cash to low-income families. Rather than putting the money in the hands of a man, the program gives a woman in the family control, empowering Pakistani women to become decision makers and advocate for their daughters' education.

Female of Firsts:
Kim Campbell (1947–)

Kim Campbell served as the prime minister of Canada for only four months, but her short stint didn't limit her accomplishments. Campbell can claim credit for a number of firsts: She was the first female prime minister of Canada, the first female minister of justice and attorney general of Canada, the first female minister of national defense, and the first woman elected to lead Canada's Progressive Conservative Party.

During her time in politics, Campbell fought for tougher gun control and passed legislation protecting women's rights. But the public was unhappy with many of her party's policies and the state of the country, which was suffering from an economic recession. Four months after her election, she stepped down as prime minister. Campbell left politics and returned to her academic roots as a university lecturer, public speaker, and member of several advisory boards.

COMMANDING KINGS
In Britain's Finest Hour
Winston Churchill (1874–1965)

In 1940, Britain was about to face the full military might of Nazi Germany. The Nazis had conquered most of Western Europe in a short amount of time, and Churchill was determined that Britain wouldn't be next. He rallied his countrymen to face their enemy through the force of his personality, delivering some of history's most inspiring speeches. The Battle of Britain—the world's first all-air battle—commenced that summer. Wave after wave of German fighter planes and bombers clashed with Royal Air Force (RAF) fighters in the skies over England. British Spitfire and German Bf 109 aircraft fell to earth riddled with bullet holes as British citizens hid in bomb shelters and underground in subway tunnels. Though Germany had more combat aircraft, the RAF managed to hold them off, and Churchill strove to keep up morale. After three months of constant air combat, the RAF emerged victorious. "Never in the field of human conflict was so much owed by so many to so few," Churchill said of his country's brave pilots.

Wilma Mankiller

≈ A Legacy of Leadership ≈

"Prior to my election, young Cherokee girls would never have thought that they might grow up and become chief."
—*Wilma Mankiller*

When the Cherokee leader Attakullakulla (AT-ta-COO-la-COO-la) traveled to negotiate trade agreements with the leaders of South Carolina in 1757, he was surprised to find that there were no women among them. Unlike European countries, the Cherokee Nation had passed power from mother to daughter for centuries. Women had long been considered equals to men, and they often held leadership roles. Wilma Mankiller brought that tradition into modern times when she became the first female to be elected chief of a major contemporary American Indian tribe.

TEARS TO TRIBAL LEADER

Wilma Mankiller was born in 1945 in Tahlequah, a city in Cherokee County, Oklahoma. Her great-grandfather had been one of the 16,000 Cherokee forced by the United States government to leave the land their ancestors had occupied for generations and walk thousands of miles to a new "Indian Territory." This brutal and often deadly journey became known as the Trail of Tears.

Royal Rundown

❀ **BORN:** November 18, 1945, Tahlequah, Oklahoma, U.S.A. ❀ **DIED:** April 6, 2010, Adair County, Oklahoma, U.S.A. ❀ **LED:** The Cherokee Nation ❀ **REMEMBERED FOR:** Becoming the first modern female chief of a Native American tribe

As chief of the Cherokee Nation from 1985 to 1995, Mankiller tripled the number of people enrolled in the tribe, doubled their employment, and constructed new housing, health care centers, and children's programs. To do it, she skillfully controlled hundreds of millions of dollars of federal funding for her tribe. Mankiller's leadership made the Cherokee Nation a national example of social and financial strength.

Poor health prevented Mankiller from running again after her third term, but she remained a strong voice for her people. In 1998, she was awarded the Presidential Medal of Freedom, the highest honor a civilian can earn in the United States. In her autobiography, Mankiller said she wanted to be remembered as someone who thought traditional Cherokee values could help solve the problems of the modern world.

Mankiller's family struggled to make ends meet. Her childhood home had no electricity, indoor plumbing, or telephones. When she was 11 years old, her family moved to San Francisco, California, as part of a government project designed to get Native Americans out of protected reservations and into America's big cities. Being forced to leave her homeland was hard on young Mankiller. She later described the journey as "my own little Trail of Tears."

Mankiller's life changed when, in 1969, she witnessed a group of young Native Americans taking over Alcatraz Island, off the coast of San Francisco, and claiming the island in the name of all Native Americans— an act designed to draw the public's attention to the government's poor treatment of tribal people. Mankiller began taking night classes to educate herself and started becoming involved in tribal affairs.

CHIEF OF A NATION

In 1981, Mankiller founded a new part of the Cherokee Nation government aimed at community development. As director, she helped set up programs to bring water to rural areas and rehabilitate dilapidated housing. Her efforts were so successful that the tribe's principal chief asked her to be his running mate when he ran for reelection in 1983. Two years later, she succeeded him as the principal chief, and she was reelected twice.

COMMANDING KINGS

Native American Hero

Hiawatha (ca 1450)

A thousand years ago in what is now New York, U.S.A., the Iroquois people began to drift apart. They broke into separate groups and settled a vast area stretching from the Great Lakes almost to the Atlantic Ocean, and fighting broke out among them. Some spiritual leaders called for peace, but few listened—except for Hiawatha. Born to the Iroquois group called the Onondaga people, Hiawatha devoted his life to traveling from chief to chief making the case for unification. According to Iroquois legend, the last holdouts were the Seneca people. As the story goes, the day they agreed to finally put down their bows, there was a solar eclipse—an event the Seneca believed was a sign that they should join the league. (Scientists have confirmed that a total solar eclipse really did occur on June 28, 1451.) United by their national hero, Hiawatha, the "five fires" of the Iroquois Confederacy began an age of peace that lasted for the next five centuries.

The Art of the Crown

FIT FOR A Queen

Not all queens sit upon a throne—or wear the headpiece to match. But one of the most famous royal headpieces in the world, the Imperial State Crown, has been a symbol of the British monarchy for generations. Designed to impress, it is the first sparkling circlet a new monarch dons during her coronation ceremony. Read on for some fancy facts about this over-the-top topper and true work of art.

Royally Remade

An earlier version of the crown was destroyed when the British monarchy was overthrown in the 17th century. When the monarchy was restored in 1660, a new crown was designed, and it's been remade about 10 times since. The queen might be secretly thankful she doesn't have to wear the original—the old sparkler weighed a whopping 7 pounds 6 ounces (3.3 kg)!

Serious Security

When it's not on the queen's head, the crown is stored safely at the Tower of London, a castle that once held famous prisoners like Queen Elizabeth I (p. 12) and Lady Jane Grey (p. 58). It's on display there for tourists to ooh and aah at as the centerpiece of the Crown Jewels exhibit.

Trial Run

The queen usually wears the crown once a year when she leads the State Opening of Parliament in London. But keeping the 2.3-pound (1-kg) crown rock-steady requires some royal skills. The queen likes to prepare by wearing the crown around Buckingham Palace in the days before the ceremony.

Top Spot

Atop the front cross is a 170-carat red spinel, a type of gem, called the Black Prince's Ruby. Look closely and you might spot a small hole where the stone was once pierced so it could be worn as a pendant. Later, the hole was plugged with a smaller stone.

Giant Gem

The royal headgear's crowning jewel is the massive diamond Cullinan II. It was cut from a stone discovered in Africa in 1905 weighing an astounding 3,107 carats—more than a pound (.62 kg)!

Spectacular Sparkle

Every nook and cranny of the Imperial State Crown is decked out in precious stones. It has four rubies, 11 emeralds, 17 sapphires, 269 pearls, and 2,868 diamonds.

Headpiece History

The crown was based on one designed for the coronation of Queen Victoria (p. 13) in 1838.

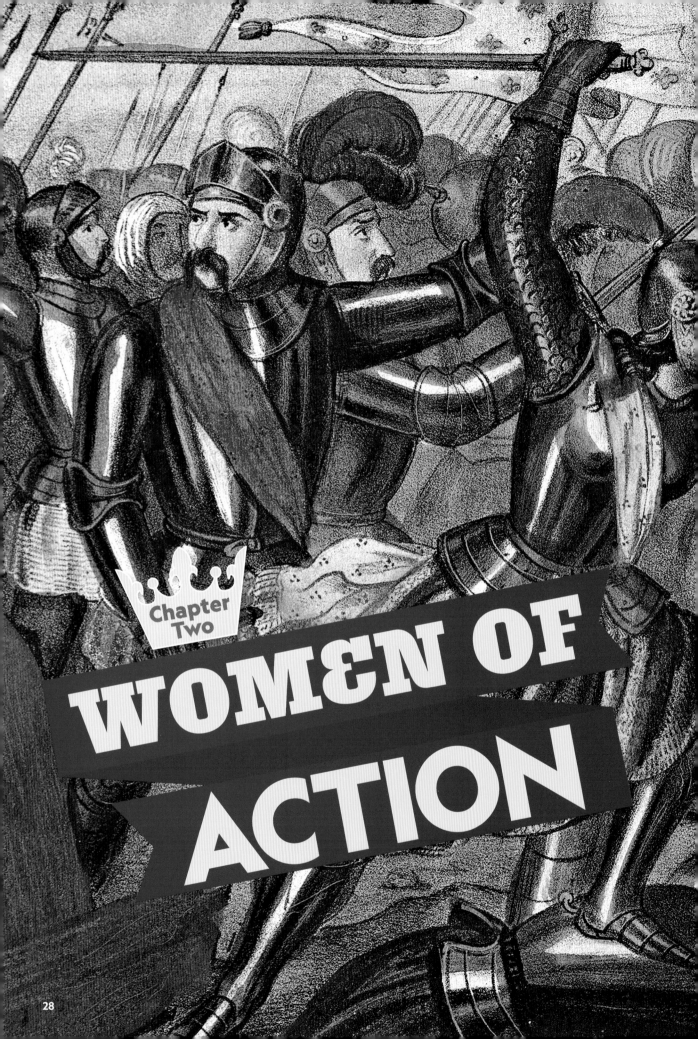

Chapter Two

WOMEN OF ACTION

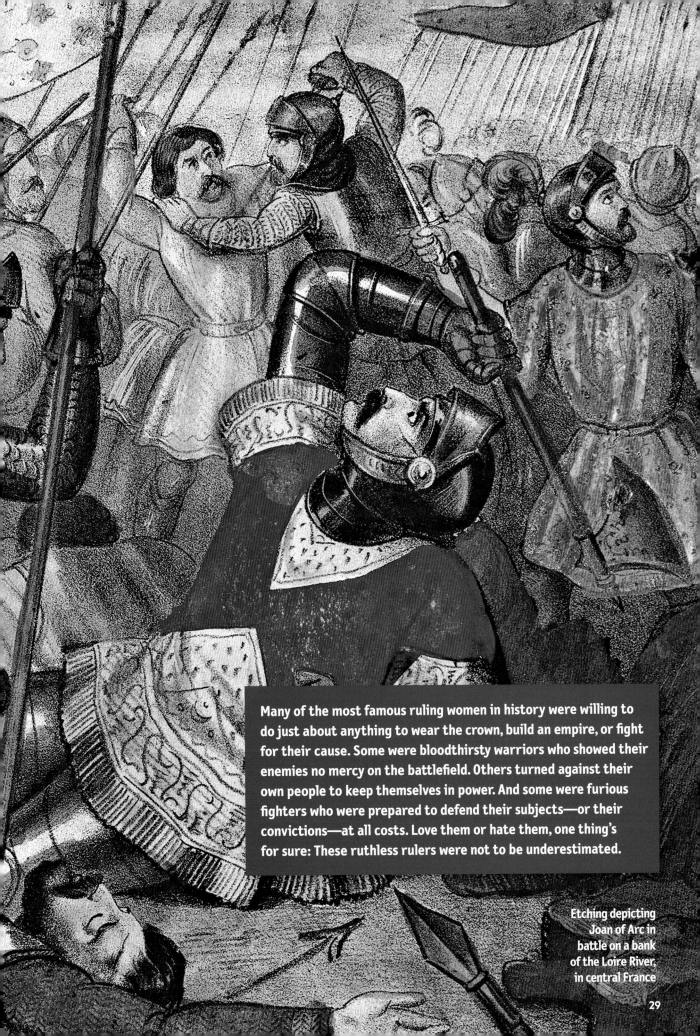

Many of the most famous ruling women in history were willing to do just about anything to wear the crown, build an empire, or fight for their cause. Some were bloodthirsty warriors who showed their enemies no mercy on the battlefield. Others turned against their own people to keep themselves in power. And some were furious fighters who were prepared to defend their subjects—or their convictions—at all costs. Love them or hate them, one thing's for sure: These ruthless rulers were not to be underestimated.

Etching depicting Joan of Arc in battle on a bank of the Loire River, in central France

Isabella I

~ Anything for an Empire ~

She united her country and financed Christopher Columbus's voyages of discovery. She made Spain a global power and created a golden age of painting, music, and literature. But there was a darker side to Queen Isabella of Spain, too: She began the brutal Spanish Inquisition, during which tens of thousands of her subjects were tortured, even killed, for freethinking and scientific progress. Today, Isabella is remembered as one of history's most influential—and controversial—leaders.

PARTNERS IN POWER

From a young age, Isabella was fiercely dedicated to climbing to the top. Laws forbade women from ruling, and she had two brothers ahead of her in line for the throne. Spain's nobility hated Isabella's much older half brother, Henry IV, the king. They backed her younger brother, Alfonso, as the rightful ruler of the historical Spanish region of Castile.

When Alfonso died at age 14, the nobles were forced to turn to Isabella. But she knew that unless King Henry recognized her as heir to the throne over his own daughter, Juana, she would probably never rule. So in a surprise strategic move, she refused to claim the throne. She acknowledged Henry as the rightful king—and in turn, he recognized her as the heir to the throne, ahead of Juana. To control his new ally, Henry then tried to set up a marriage for Isabella with a man of his choosing— but Isabella wouldn't be trapped. While pretending to go along with his plan, she secretly married a man she picked instead: Ferdinand, heir to the throne of Aragon. When Henry died in 1474, 23-year-old Isabella took the crown as queen of Castile.

Queen Isabella I was the first woman featured on United States postage stamps.

Royal Rundown

❀ **BORN:** April 22, 1451, Madrigal de las Altas Torres, Spain ❀ **DIED:** November 26, 1504, Medina del Campo, Spain ❀ **LED:** Spain ❀ **REMEMBERED FOR:** Uniting Spain

QUEEN OF A NEW WORLD

When Isabella came to power, Spain was made up of multiple kingdoms warring for dominance. Isabella and Ferdinand's marriage made the territories of Aragon and Castile into one—but that wasn't enough for the queen. She wanted to rule an empire.

Granada, today a province of southern Spain, was under control of the Moors, a nomadic people from northern Africa. Isabella sent her armies to seize the territory, calling the fight a Christian crusade. They took control of Granada in 1492, and the country of Spain was finally united. But the wars had emptied the royal treasury. If Isabella wanted her new empire to survive, she needed to find a way to fill it— and quickly. So she made the decision that would make her famous: She sent Christopher Columbus west to find a quicker route to India and Asia, where highly prized spices were grown. Though he didn't find India, he did find North America—the New World. Isabella's territory now extended beyond Spain's borders.

CRUEL RULER

Shrewd and savvy, Isabella knew that as the only female ruler of the 15th century, her hold on the monarchy was unsteady. She carefully constructed an image of herself as a quiet woman who always deferred to her male advisers and spent her days devoting herself to her religion, Catholicism.

Some historians think Isabella was truly religious; others think she just used her faith as a tool to attain power. Spain's subjects were Christian, Islamic, and Jewish—but Isabella was intent on uniting her country not only as one nation but also under one faith. She and Ferdinand decreed that everyone who was not a Christian must leave Spain. Isabella began the infamous Spanish Inquisition, which used extreme methods, including torture, to "prove" that people were still practicing their faiths in secret—then burned them at the stake. Before long, the ruthless Inquisition was hunting down anyone deemed an enemy of the empire.

For the price of thousands of her people's lives, Isabella succeeded in uniting Spain and turning it into a player on the world stage. Her grandson Charles V inherited territory that included Spain, the Netherlands, Luxembourg, Sardinia, Sicily, Naples, South America, and the West Indies—a true empire.

The marriage of Isabella and Ferdinand united Spain's two most powerful kingdoms, but that was only the beginning of their empire.

King of the New World?
Christopher Columbus's Expedition

He's honored with a United States holiday celebrating his arrival in the Americas on October 12, 1492. But does Christopher Columbus deserve to be celebrated? Many history books teach that he discovered North America. But—besides the fact that millions of indigenous people were living there long before Columbus sailed the ocean blue— the truth is that the explorer never actually set foot on the continent. Instead, he spent eight years bouncing around between the islands of the Caribbean and the coast of South America. He never figured out where he was, stubbornly insisting that he'd found a westward route to Asia, as he'd set out to do. Like many explorers of the time, he exploited, attacked, and enslaved the native people he encountered. Eventually, his conduct caught up with him. The Spanish government stripped Columbus of his power and brought him back to Spain in chains.

PIRATE QUEENS

❧ *They Ruled the High Seas* ❧

Today, pirates might seem like the stuff of stories. But in the ancient world, pirates really did pillage and plunder. Nearly all were men: In fact, an old sailing superstition told that a woman would doom any ship she set foot upon. But these women climbed aboard anyway and became some of the fiercest buccaneers to ever sail the seven seas.

Terror of the Mediterranean:
Queen Teuta of Illyria (ca 200 B.C.)

The mighty ships of the Roman Republic ruled the Mediterranean Sea in 241 B.C. But there was trouble on the horizon in the form of Teuta, queen of a fearsome people called the Illyrians, in what is today the Western Balkans (a region in southeastern Europe). The Illyrians practiced piracy and they were proud of it, and Teuta supported her people. So when two Roman ambassadors tried to negotiate with her to put a stop to piracy, she refused. The ambassadors sailed for home, but one was killed on the return trip—maybe on Teuta's orders, maybe not. The Romans were furious. They declared war against the Illyrians. Though Rome eventually did take over her lands and put an end to buccaneering, Teuta made sure the pirates didn't go down without a fight.

A Pirate's Life for Her:
Anne Bonny (ca 1698–1782)

Women living in the American colonial era didn't have much of a say in whom they would marry. Parents usually chose a suitable suitor and that was that. But when young Anne's father betrothed her to a man in what is now Charleston, South Carolina, Anne couldn't bear to face a life of laundry and child rearing. So she ran away from home, boarded a ship for the Bahamas, and met infamous pirate "Calico Jack" Rackham. Anne discovered her talent for piracy. She would don trousers, a sword, and a brace of pistols on her hip, joining the crew as they hijacked trade ships for their goods. When one crew member protested that there was a female on the ship, legend says that Bonny attacked him—and no one ever brought it up again.

Dressed as a Man:
Mary Read (1685–1721)

Anne Bonny started out the lone woman on her ship—but it didn't stay that way. Somewhere in the West Indies, Anne and her crew took over another vessel. When Bonny taunted one captive, the prisoner revealed in secret that she too was a woman, her gender disguised so she could sail. That woman, Mary Read, swore Anne to secrecy and joined Calico Jack's crew. During battles, Anne and Mary fought side by side. They wore long trousers, wrapped handkerchiefs around their heads, and brandished a pistol in one hand and a machete in the other. On October 22, 1720, a vessel sailed up alongside Calico Jack's ship. Calico Jack signaled his surrender, but Anne and Mary refused. They remained on deck and faced their enemies alone. Legend says that Mary was so outraged at the crew's cowardice that she stopped firing long enough to yell into the hold, "If there's a man among ye, ye'll come up and fight like the man ye are to be!

Queen of All Pirates:
Ching Shih (1775–1844)

The most successful pirate of all time wasn't Blackbeard or Captain Kidd. It was Ching Shih, a powerful female pirate who came to control not just one ship but an entire fleet. When Shih, as a young woman, married the Chinese pirate captain Cheng in 1801, she made him a deal: She would be his bride, but he had to treat her as an equal. So the husband-and-wife pirate team sailed along the coast of the South China Sea, picking off ships. When Cheng died in 1807, Shih took total control. She named her husband's second-in-command, Chang Pao, captain of her fleet and sent him off to pillage while she took care of the business side of the operation: recruiting more pirates. Soon, Shih controlled nearly all the piracy in the region and commanded a fleet of more than 1,500 ships and 80,000 outlaws.

Marauder of the Irish Coast:
Grace O'Malley (1530–1603)

Born to a wealthy Irish seafaring family in 1530, Grace O'Malley rejected the life of the average 16th-century woman in favor of adventure on the high seas. Her father owned large territories of coastal land and taxed fishermen who used his waters. When he died, O'Malley took over—and took things to the next level. She built a fleet and started collecting taxes and tolls on every ship she could find. If people refused to pay up, O'Malley became violent. Before long, she was a full-on pirate with an empire of land and ships at her disposal. O'Malley spent the rest of her life striking terror into anyone who sailed too close. In the 1580s, when an English lord captured her son in a raid, O'Malley personally sailed to England to ask Queen Elizabeth I (p. 12) to give him back. She refused to bow and even tried to sneak a dagger into the meeting. Perhaps impressed by a female ruler as strong as she, Elizabeth agreed to his release.

Phoolan Devi

⚜ The "Bandit Queen" ⚜

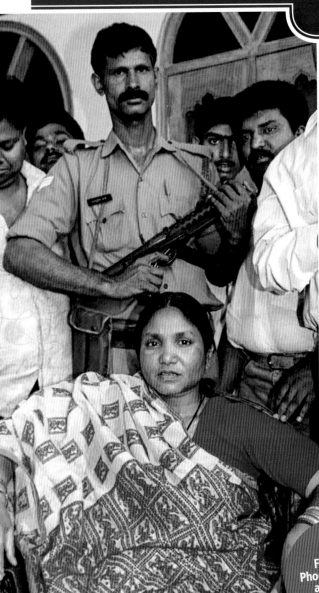

For a time, Phoolan Devi had a bounty on her head.

Some think Phoolan Devi, nicknamed the "Bandit Queen" of India, was a real-life Robin Hood who helped those who needed it most. Others believe her acts of vicious vengeance make her little more than a criminal.

Devi was born into a poor family belonging to one of India's lowest castes, or classes. When she was 11, her family arranged for her to marry a violent man three times her age—in exchange for a cow. When she managed to escape her abusive marriage, her family considered her a disgrace to their name. By the time she was in her early 20s, Devi had been dragged through the underbelly of Indian society until she finally decided she had had enough. She rallied a group of rebel bandits around her and enacted her revenge. Devi and her gang captured towns, looted their goods and gave them away to the poor. They attacked and killed Devi's former abusers. Devi became a wanted criminal—and also a cult hero. Many saw her acts of revenge as an attack on India's evil upper castes.

Devi was imprisoned for 11 years, but her story was far from over. Two years after she was released, she exchanged bullets for ballots and took advantage of her fame to run for office as a member of the Samajwadi Party. She won the 1996 elections and served as a member of parliament. During her second term, Devi was returning home from her government office when three masked men opened fire on Devi and her bodyguard. She died on July 25 2001. Though she was ruthless in her pursuit of revenge, Devi was a symbol of resistance many Indians still revere today. Her life has inspired dozens of books, films and even an opera.

Royal Rundown

❀ **BORN:** August 10, 1963, Ghura Ka Purwa, Uttar Pradesh, India   ❀ **DIED:** July 25, 2001, New Delhi, India
❀ **LED:** A movement for change in India   ❀ **REMEMBERED FOR:** Her efforts to help India's lower castes

Queen Tomyris

❦ Savage Sovereign ❦

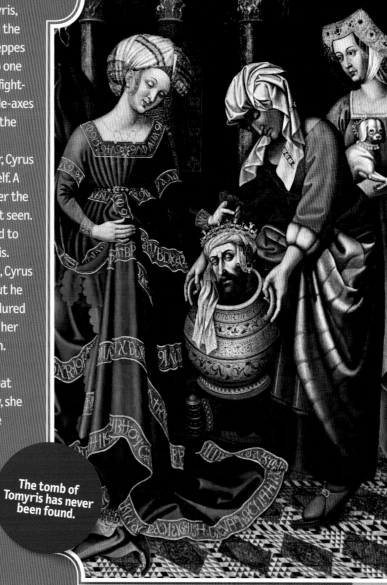

The tomb of Tomyris has never been found.

Facts muddle with fiction in the tale of Tomyris, an ancient queen who ruled a people called the Massagetae, nomads who wandered the steppes near present-day Kazakhstan. According to one historian's account, the Massagetae were ferocious fighters who rode into battle on horseback carrying battle-axes made of brass. And if the legends are to be believed, the fiercest of them all was Queen Tomyris.

Her road to fame began when a neighboring ruler, Cyrus the Great, decided he wanted her kingdom for himself. A warrior king, Cyrus had led military conquests all over the region and built the largest empire the world had yet seen. Tomyris's territory was next on his list. First, he tried to take control by proposing marriage to Queen Tomyris. When she saw through his plan and turned him down, Cyrus got angry. He gathered his army and declared war. But he didn't fight with honor: Cyrus staged a banquet and lured Tomyris's troops there—only to slaughter a third of her soldiers. While he was at it, he captured Tomyris's son.

Tomyris attacked with the full fury of her fierce fighters—and she led them into battle herself. In what one historian called the most violent clash in history, she killed Cyrus and destroyed his army. That's where the tale gets even more gruesome: According to some accounts, she then beheaded her enemy and used his skull as a drinking goblet. Whether that part of the story is true or just a tall tale, Tomyris will always be remembered as the queen who defeated the most powerful army on Earth.

Royal Rundown

❀ **LIVED:** ca 6th century B.C., Central Asia ❀ **LED:** The Massagetae
❀ **REMEMBERED FOR:** Defeating the most powerful king in the world

WARRIOR QUEENS

❧ *Bravery on the Battlefield* ❧

These were queens to be reckoned with. They led their countries through wars, invasions, and conflict. And when times got really tough, they weren't afraid to get their hands dirty: These women took up arms and led their troops to victory.

The Queen Who Changed History: Æthelflæd of Mercia (ca 870–918)

Times were turbulent in the late 9th and early 10th centuries in Britain. Danish warriors had landed in the east and were toppling kings and taking over castles. England seemed ready to fall. So it was bad timing when the king of Mercia, the most powerful kingdom of the Anglo-Saxon era, fell ill and died in 911. With battles all around them and no one else to turn to, the people were forced to recognize his wife, Æthelflæd (ATH-el-flad), as monarch. Æthelflæd built a protective network of nine forts to keep Mercia safe from invaders. She beat back the Danish armies, who not only surrendered but also swore to be her loyal subjects. Without her skillful leadership, England very likely would have ended up in different hands. Most extraordinary of all, when Æthelflæd died, in 918, her daughter, Ælfwynn, stepped onto the throne in her place. It was the first time the crown had passed from woman to woman in Europe, and it wouldn't happen again in Britain for almost 600 years.

A Ruler to Remember: Amanitore (ca 1 B.C.–ca A.D. 20)

Amanitore was a warrior queen so mighty that she earned a mention in the Bible. Her kingdom was Nubia, a region along the Nile River between what is today Sudan and Egypt. She ruled one of the oldest civilizations of ancient Africa, which dates back to at least 2000 B.C. Amanitore was the descendant of female monarchs known for their bravery on the battlefield, and she followed in their fearsome footsteps, leading her forces into battle herself. But Amanitore didn't just fight: She was also one of the greatest builders of her time. Under her instruction, temples were built and restored, and reservoirs were constructed to ensure her people had water during dry seasons. During her rule, more than 200 Nubian pyramids were built——many of which still survive today.

Queen of the Desert: Mavia of Arabia
(ca A.D. 375)

No evidence of her existence remains in the desert land where she ruled. But songs and stories passed down from generation to generation have preserved the tale of one of Arabia's most famous queens. Around A.D. 375, she likely became a queen when she married the leader of the Tanukh tribe that inhabited what is today southern Palestine and the northern Sinai Peninsula. Mavia lived a life on the move: She slept under the stars and rode her horse across the dunes. Her skills on horseback came in handy when her husband died and

Emperor Valens, leader of the Romans who were invading the area, thought her tribe would be an easy target. He was wrong. Mavia guided her people to disappear into the desert. From there, she led her cavalry in attacks on Roman troops. The men she faced on the battlefield didn't take her seriously, something the warrior queen used to her advantage as she won fight after fight. Soon, the Romans had to admit that they'd underestimated her. They surrendered, and Mavia forced them to sign a peace treaty on her terms.

Mighty General: Fu Hao (ca 1250 B.C.)

For thousands of years, people have been telling the story of Lady Fu Hao, the first female general ever to live in China. But many thought she was nothing more than a myth until 1976, when her tomb was discovered on the outskirts of Anyang, in China's Henan Province. Buried alongside her were weapons, mirrors, pottery, 440 bronze vessels, hundreds of hairpins, pieces of jade, and the remains of 16 slaves meant to take care of her in the afterlife. It was highly unusual for a woman in ancient China to be given such an elaborate burial. But Fu Hao was highly unusual herself: She was the wife of the king Wu Ding of the Shang dynasty that ruled China from about 1600 to 1046 B.C., around the same time as the great pharaohs of Egypt. And she used that position to lead an army of 13,000 soldiers, the king's largest. She also advised the king on political matters, predicted the future by reading oracles, and led religious rites. Wu Ding so valued his wife's opinion that after she died, he made sacrifices in her honor, asking for her guidance from beyond the grave.

Mean Queens

Fairy-tale princesses are sweet, kind, and always do the right thing. But the rulers of their famous fables? They're a different story. Meet four of the meanest queens who ever made a wicked potion or cast a nefarious spell.

The Evil Queen From *Snow White*

So wicked she doesn't have a name, the Evil Queen from the 1937 film *Snow White*, inspired by an 1812 fairy tale published by the Grimm brothers, is Disney's first—and possibly worst—villain. The queen is chillingly beautiful, and she knows it. Obsessed with remaining the fairest in the land, she regularly consults her magic mirror to make sure she still holds the title. So when the mirror declares Snow White to be the fairest of them all, the Evil Queen is enraged. She sets off to take back what she thinks is rightfully hers. Disguising herself as an old woman, she carries a poisoned apple to Snow White's cottage and tricks the girl into taking a bite. In the end, love's true kiss saves the princess—who then secures her place as fairest in the land when the mean queen tumbles off a cliff to her demise.

The Queen of Hearts From *Alice's Adventures in Wonderland*

"Off with their heads!" is this maniacal monarch's favorite phrase. The Queen of Hearts is the ruling villain in *Alice's Adventures in Wonderland*, a novel by 19th-century English author Lewis Carroll. Short-tempered and prone to tantrums, the Queen of Hearts insists on getting her way—and she doesn't apologize for it. Her subjects might respond to her every request with a quick "Yes, Your Majesty," but if they commit an error she sees as unforgivable—such as planting roses of the wrong color—it's time for a beheading!

Ursula From *The Little Mermaid*

Half woman, half octopus, and all trouble, Ursula is the dark queen of the sea in the 1989 Disney film *The Little Mermaid*, based on an 1837 fairy tale by Hans Christian Andersen. Unlike other mean queens, who pick a fight with a princess, Ursula's beef is with King Triton, the ruler of their underwater world. When his daughter Ariel comes along, singing sad songs and mooning around wishing she lived somewhere besides her palace under the sea, Ursula sees an opportunity. Pretending to only want to help, the octo-witch conjures up a pair of legs for the hapless mermaid so that she can pursue Eric, her landlocked love. The price for this gift? Ariel has to give up her voice. Of course, it was all part of Ursula's doomed scam to take the kingdom.

Maleficent From *Sleeping Beauty*

This malicious fairy—aptly named Maleficent—calls herself the "mistress of all evil" in the classic 1959 animated Disney film *Sleeping Beauty*, from a story originally published by French author Charles Perrault in 1696. When she's not invited to the christening of the newborn Princess Aurora, Maleficent takes out her anger by cursing the innocent baby. She tricks Aurora into pricking her finger on a spinning wheel, and the princess falls into a deep sleep. When a prince comes to rescue her, Maleficent transforms herself into a truly impressive alter ego: a giant, fire-breathing dragon. Naturally, the hero slays the dragon to rescue the princess—waking her with a kiss—but the evil fairy doesn't go down without a fight.

Mary I

∾ Bloody Mary ∾

England's first female monarch, Mary I, ruled for just five years. Her story is packed with warring siblings, power-hungry nobles, and even evil stepmothers. As a child, Mary was little more than a pawn offered in marriage to curry favor with nobles of other countries. As queen, her political policies failed. Yet Mary left her mark on history—and earned the nickname "Bloody Mary"—because of the ruthless persecution of those who didn't share her religious beliefs.

PRINCESS TO POWERLESS

Mary was the only child of Queen Catherine of Aragon (daughter of Spanish monarchs King Ferdinand II and Queen Isabella [p. 30]) and Henry VIII, a king best known for beheading a series of wives. At first, Henry viewed Mary as a negotiating tool he could use to increase his power by marrying her off to the right noble. But when Catherine didn't have any more children, Henry saw both his wife and daughter as obstacles in the way of his true goal: a male heir.

After becoming infatuated with one of the maids of honor in Catherine's court, Anne Boleyn, Henry petitioned Catherine for a divorce. But divorce was not only against Catherine's faith; she knew that splitting from her husband would destroy Mary's royal future. She fought back fiercely and got the pope on her side. The pope denied Henry's request to end the marriage through the church.

Henry, determined to get his way regardless, broke ties with the Catholic Church for the first time in England's history. In 1533, he started his own religion, the Church of England, and declared

Royal Rundown

❀ **BORN:** February 18, 1516, Greenwich, England
❀ **DIED:** November 17, 1558, London, England
❀ **LED:** England ❀ **REMEMBERED FOR:** Seizing the crown for herself

his marriage to Catherine invalid. That began the religious divide that would later nearly destroy England—with Mary at the helm.

BECOMING QUEEN

Just as Henry had hoped, his new wife, Anne, did give birth to a child ... but she was a daughter—the future Queen Elizabeth I (p. 12). Henry demoted Mary as princess, giving the title to Elizabeth. He forced Mary to recognize him as head of the church and publicly state that his marriage to her mother, Catherine, was illegitimate. Eventually, Mary did what her father wanted. Henry allowed Mary to return to court and officially recognized her as heir behind Edward VI—the son Henry finally got after four more marriages.

When Henry died in 1547, his multiple marriages meant the line of succession to the throne was in serious turmoil. When his son Edward died at age 15 after a short reign as king, Lady Jane Grey (p. 58), the granddaughter of Henry's younger sister, took the throne in a surprise move. But Mary had the support of the people. She challenged the new queen and, at age 37, took the crown she had once been entitled to as the only child of the king.

FALL FROM THE THRONE

Now that she was queen of England, Mary became obsessed with the same problem that had plagued her father—an heir. Mary knew that unless she had a child to pass the crown to, her Protestant half sister, Elizabeth, would become queen. That wasn't acceptable to Mary,

Mary burned hundreds of people at the stake to punish them for their religious convictions, earning the royal her infamous nickname: Bloody Mary.

who was a devoted Catholic like her Spanish mother, Catherine. To convert England back to Catholicism, Mary needed a Catholic heir. So she announced that she would marry the Catholic Philip II of Spain—a decision that was extremely unpopular with her people, who feared they'd be taken over by Spain.

But Mary didn't care what her subjects wanted. She repealed many of the religious edicts her father had put in place when he started his own church and replaced them with her own. She instated laws against heresy, making it a crime to have any belief that opposed the Catholic Church. England was full of Protestants, and so Mary had plenty of "criminals" to pursue. She spent the next three years relentlessly hunting down and executing Protestants.

Mary's people turned against her. They rose up in protest against "Bloody Mary." The queen, still without an heir and now despised by her subjects, was forced to step down and allow her Protestant half sister, Elizabeth, to take the throne. To this day, Mary's reign remains one of the bloodiest, most tumultuous periods in English history.

Untangling the Tudors

The House of Tudor was the English royal dynasty that ruled England from 1485 to 1603. Here's a partial family tree showing how this complicated clan is connected (the crown icon signifies Tudor heirs to the throne):

Ferdinand II ══ Isabella I

Jane Seymour ══ Anne Boleyn ══ Henry VIII ══ Catherine of Aragon ══ Anne of Cleves / Catherine Howard / Catherine Parr

Edward VI   Elizabeth I   Mary I ══ Philip II

Catherine de Médicis

∽ Warmonger or Peacekeeper? ∿

Legend says that Catherine de Médicis introduced the fork to France.

Catherine was born to the Medici family, rulers of Florence, Italy, during much of the Italian Renaissance. At age 14, she was married off to Henry II, heir to the French throne. Catherine loved Henry, but he openly disliked her. Despite that, they managed to have 10 children together before the king was injured during a joust and died in 1559.

Upon his father's death, Catherine's son Francis II was proclaimed king. At the time, France had two warring religious groups, the Catholics and the Protestant Huguenots. The Huguenots used the transfer of power as an opportun to try to take over the royal court. The royal army put dow the rebellion, but Catherine and her sons would struggle w fighting between the two groups for the rest of their lives. Francis died less than a year after taking over, leaving the throne to Catherine's second son, Charles IX. Because Char was only 10 years old, Catherine took control of the nation She was supposed to rule only until Charles was old enough but she never gave up her power.

That's where Catherine's reputation as an evil queen rea began. She used her daughter Marguerite as a bargaining c to try to create harmony between Catholics and Protestan by brokering Marguerite's marriage to a Protestant king. When one of Catherine's enemies grew sick and died, many suspected she had actually been murdered by Catherine, wl was rumored to have an extensive collection of poisons. Anc worst of all, in 1572, Catherine persuaded Charles that the Huguenots were plotting to rise against him and that they to be stopped. At her suggestion, Charles ordered the murc of about 10,000 Huguenots. For the rest of her rule, Cather continued to use her children as political pawns and scheme against her enemies. When she died in 1589, her country was embroiled in one of the worst civil wars of its history.

Royal Run

BORN: April 13, 1519, Florence, Italy **DIED:** January 5, 1589, Blois, France
LED: France **REMEMBERED FOR:** Starting a war to keep the peace

Ranavalona I

∞ Tyrant or Traditionalist? ∞

The details about Ranavalona's life differ from story to story. Some say she was born a commoner but got a lucky break when her father uncovered a conspiracy to assassinate the king of Madagascar. The king was so happy to escape death that he arranged for Ranavalona to marry his son, Radama. After inheriting the throne, Radama died suddenly at 36. Some historians believe the cause was disease; others suppose he was poisoned by his wife.

The throne should have then gone to Radama's brother. But Ranavalona had the monarchy in her sights, and she wasn't about to let go. She seized the palace and executed the members of the royal family. In 1828, Ranavalona was crowned queen of Madagascar. Anyone suspected of opposing her was forced to take part in a bizarre and vicious ceremony: They had to eat three pieces of chicken skin, then a poisonous nut called the tangena. Only if the nut caused the suspect to vomit up all three pieces of chicken skin was he considered innocent.

Ranavalona was determined to make Madagascar self-sufficient, a kingdom that could survive without trading goods or requesting aid from other countries. When a French fortune hunter named Jean Laborde swam ashore after being shipwrecked in 1831, Ranavalona recognized his engineering and munitions skills and took him into her inner circle. She directed Laborde to set up a factory to produce everything the people would need, from guns to soap. Ranavalona banned Christianity, and the missionaries who had been on Madagascar for decades hid or fled. When French and English armies attacked in 1849, Ranavalona destroyed them and then mounted 21 of the soldiers' skulls on the shore as a warning to future invaders.

> "Never say, 'she is only a feeble and ignorant woman, how can she rule such a vast empire?' I will rule here, to the good fortune of my people and the glory of my name!"
> —*Ranavalona I*

Royal Rundown

❀ **BORN:** 1778 ❀ **DIED:** August 16, 1861, Madagascar ❀ **LED:** Madagascar
❀ **REMEMBERED FOR:** Seizing an opportunity to take over the throne

ROYAL PAINS

❧ *Women Who Wreaked Havoc* ❧

Not all the people on these pages were queens themselves—but they were royal annoyances to the monarchs in charge. From a woman who causes chaos in a classic tale to a real-life girl whose bold moves started a war, these women were nothing but bad news for those who sat on the throne.

The Girl Who Started a War: Joan of Arc (1412–1431)

Warrior, saint—and a major pain to King Henry V of England—Joan of Arc became an unlikely hero to France. It all started when, at 13, she started hearing voices in her head that she was sure came from God. The voices told Joan to cut her hair, dress in men's clothing, and go persuade the French king Charles VII to take back his land from English rule. She must have made a convincing case, because Charles listened to the unknown girl and sent his troops into battle, with Joan at their head. The French Army beat the English into retreat and restored control of France. But the English and King Henry V never forgave Joan for ripping their conquered land away from them. When she was just 19, English soldiers captured her, accused her of being a witch, and burned her at the stake. Joan's bravery in standing up to Henry and the English army is still celebrated today.

The Classic Villain: Lady Macbeth

Lady Macbeth is a main character in William Shakespeare's play *Macbeth*, first performed around 1606. The story starts out happy. Macbeth, a soldier returning from battle, comes across three witches who tell his fortune: He's going to become royalty. Not one to leave her future to chance, Lady Macbeth—his wife—decides to take fortune into her own hands. She talks her husband into killing Duncan, the king of Scotland, so that he can be the king and she the queen. The act sends Lady Macbeth on a slow slide into murder and madness that comes together to make Shakespeare's bloodiest—and some say most brilliant—work.

The Terror of Mount Olympus: Hera

In Greek mythology, Hera was the queen of all gods, goddesses, and mortals on Earth. But it wasn't enough for Hera, who spent her life getting revenge on whomever she decided had wronged her. Famously jealous, she was always raising thunderstorms or banishing her husband, Zeus (p. 121), from Mount Olympus. When Zeus fell in love with a maiden named Io, Hera got revenge by turning the girl into a cow. When the hero Hercules was born, the furious Hera sent snakes to kill the baby—her first of many attempts to end his life. Hera was vengeful; for this reason, Greek women who hoped to punish their husbands for misdeeds would pray to her. Hera's personality made her one of ancient Greece's most popular goddesses.

The Face That Launched a Thousand Ships: Helen of Troy

This legendary lady of Greek myth was called the most beautiful woman in the world. But her beauty would prove to be nothing but trouble for many people in ancient Greece, especially Priam, the king of Troy, and Menelaus, the king of Sparta. From a gaggle of suitors, Helen picked Menelaus to be her husband. Around this time, Greece's three major goddesses—Hera, Athena, and Aphrodite—were embroiled in a bitter rivalry over who was the most beautiful. Determined to win at all costs, Aphrodite bribed the judge, Paris, by offering him the most beautiful mortal woman in the world as his wife. It worked. Aphrodite kept her promise and made Helen fall in love with Paris, who stole her away from Sparta in his ship and sailed home to Troy. When Menelaus found his new wife was gone, he was so furious that he marched into battle against Paris—beginning the famous Trojan War.

COMMANDING KINGS

Europe's Troublemaker

Napoleon Bonaparte (1769–1821)

When the French Revolution began in 1789, the people, tired of being bossed around by selfish monarchs, had big dreams of democracy. They hoped for a republic in which people had equal rights and freedom of speech and religion. What they got instead was a dictator: Napoleon Bonaparte. After rising rapidly through the ranks of the French military during the revolution, Napoleon seized power and crowned himself emperor in 1804. Once in charge, he proved himself a major thorn in the side of neighboring rulers, declaring war on Britain, Austria, and Russia. One of history's greatest military leaders, Napoleon expanded France into an empire that, in 1811, controlled much of Europe. Eventually, however, Napoleon was defeated and died in exile on the island of St. Helena. Even though he was a dictator, Napoleon wrote a civil code that laid out many revolutionary ideals, including establishing equality before the law and guaranteeing individual liberty. It lived beyond him, sparking the principles of democracy across Europe.

Ironclad Maidens

FIT FOR A Queen

We know some queens of the past rode fearlessly into battle, wielding weapons and leading troops to victory. Though a medieval military was made mostly of men, a few notable women took up arms, too. And, just like their male counterparts, they wore protective armor on the battlefield. What do we know about them?

Legendary Look

Many images of armor-clad women from the past depict fictional figures, like Minerva, the Roman goddess of women and warfare. According to legend, when Minerva's mother, Metis, was pregnant with her, Minerva's father, Jupiter, swallowed Metis because of a prophecy that their child would grow up to defeat him. While in Jupiter's stomach, Metis forged weapons for her baby. The constant hammering of metal gave Jupiter such a headache that he asked another god to strike his forehead with a hammer. It split open, and Minerva emerged, grown and in full battle armor.

Armor for All

The scarce historical accounts of women in battle tell that, when arming themselves, they likely donned the same gear as the men. They're usually described as wearing hauberks, garments made of chain mail that covered the arms, torso, and upper legs. Of course, many topped off the look with a sword and shield. *Charge!*

Custom Fit

Joan of Arc (p. 44) is one of history's most famous warrior women. It is said that King Charles VII ordered a suit of armor made to fit her perfectly. Now that's personal protection!

Knight Me

In 1149, when invaders threatened to take over the town of Tortosa, Spain, the local women threw on men's clothing, grabbed whatever sharp and heavy objects they could find, and fought off the enemy. Spanish count Ramon Berenguer IV was so impressed that he created the Order of the Hatchet, granting the brave women rights similar to those of knights.

Secret Suit

Though plenty of old paintings depict women in mail armor and metal plates, there are no known images of a woman in armor that were made during that woman's lifetime. That means the exact appearance of women's armor is still a mystery.

"Womanly" Weapons

Sometimes, artists' portrayals of women on the battlefield didn't get the facts quite right. Many medieval manuscripts that depict women fighting don't show them carrying lances—which were considered weapons for men. Instead, the artists picture their female fighters wielding distaffs—tools used for spinning fibers into fabric!

Limestone carving of Egyptian ruler Nefertiti with her husband, Akhenaten, and their children

Chapter Three

REVOLUTIONARY RULERS

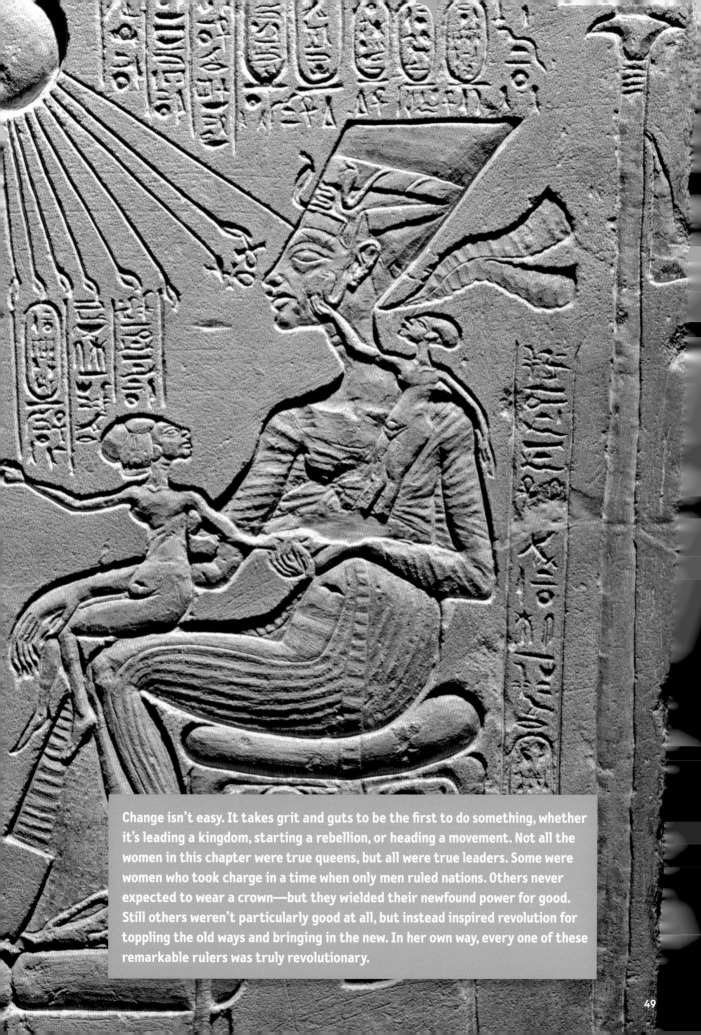

Change isn't easy. It takes grit and guts to be the first to do something, whether it's leading a kingdom, starting a rebellion, or heading a movement. Not all the women in this chapter were true queens, but all were true leaders. Some were women who took charge in a time when only men ruled nations. Others never expected to wear a crown—but they wielded their newfound power for good. Still others weren't particularly good at all, but instead inspired revolution for toppling the old ways and bringing in the new. In her own way, every one of these remarkable rulers was truly revolutionary.

Christina of Sweden

∽ Learned Leader ∾

In a time when women were seen as little more than accessories meant to decorate the arms of their much more important husbands, Christina of Sweden turned everything upside down. Smart, savvy, devoted to culture and the arts—and stubbornly independent—Christina is still remembered by the people of Sweden as a monarch with a mind of her own.

THE "GIRL KING"

When Christina was born, in 1516, her parents were desperate for a male heir to take the throne. Though Swedish law didn't prevent a woman from ruling, Sweden had been at war with Poland for 26 years, and the monarchy was already in a precarious position. So King Gustavus was thrilled when the royal midwives told him his wife had finally given birth to a boy. But when it was revealed that there had been a mistake, and that the infant was a girl instead, he merely laughed and said, "She'll be a clever one—she's fooled all of us!" Gustavus kept this forward-thinking attitude as he raised his daughter. Realizing she'd likely someday be the ruler, he raised her as he would have raised a prince. She studied art, philosophy, languages, horsemanship, and war tactics—as well as ballet to learn grace. When Gustavus died in battle, Christina was only six years old—but her strong will and intelligence hinted she would someday be up to the task of leading her country. The regents who ruled in her name quickly realized what they were dealing with and began allowing Christina to attend council meetings when she was just 14. At 18 years old, she was crowned to rule in her own right.

"To obey no one is a greater happiness than to command the whole world."
—*Queen Christina*

Royal Rundown

❋ **BORN:** December 18, 1626, Stockholm, Sweden ❋ **DIED:** April 19, 1689, Rome, Italy
❋ **LED:** Sweden ❋ **REMEMBERED FOR:** Establishing peace and celebrating the arts

QUEEN OF ARTS

Christina was a lover of learning who woke up every morning at five to study before her royal duties began. She wanted to make her capital, Stockholm, the cultural center of the world—but first, she had to bring peace to her country. That wasn't an easy task: At the time, Sweden was embroiled in the Thirty Years' War with other European countries including France, Spain, Denmark, and the Holy Roman Empire. But Christina prevailed. She was a major player in brokering the peace settlement that ended the fighting. Class rivalries broke out as the war ended, but Christina was able to use her political skills to stave off civil war—though she dealt with the financial trouble caused by years of fighting for the rest of her rule.

Christina turned her attention to the arts. She had a theater and an astronomy observatory built in one of her palaces. She invited writers, musicians, and scholars to her court—including the famed French philosopher René Descartes, who started an academy there. She spent extravagantly to support these great thinkers—but Sweden didn't have the money to keep them there. Deterred by the lack of funds (and the extreme cold!), they drifted away.

Christina's power and status as a queen is symbolized by her depiction on a rearing horse.

AFTER THE REIGN

Christina loved riding and hunting, wore men's clothes, and detested anything feminine. She revealed that she had no interest in marriage—which would leave Sweden without an heir. On top of that, she had secretly converted to Catholicism—something that her Lutheran people could not accept. After 10 years of rule, Christina shocked everyone by abdicating the throne—which went to her cousin Charles Gustavus—and moving to Rome, Italy.

In spite of this scandal and the mixed successes of her rule, Christina became one of the most influential figures of her time. She spent the rest of her life supporting the arts. She managed to build a spectacular collection of paintings and other works and helped found one of Rome's earliest academic centers and its first public opera house. Her collection of books and manuscripts is now in the library of the Vatican, in Vatican City. Today, she is remembered as a truly unconventional queen.

COMMANDING KINGS

The Last of His Kind

Louis XVI (1754–1793)

Louis XVI ruled France as many kings had before him—with total power and word that was law. Unfortunately for Louis, he was also France's last absolute monarch. He ruled during the age of enlightenment, a period in which ideas like liberty and equality were becoming popular and ordinary citizens were revolting against their overbearing kings. France had just helped the British colonists in America break free from their king when the French people began clamoring for the same liberty.

On July 14, 1789, after most of the country had endured years of extreme poverty and starvation while Louis and his wife, Marie Antoinette, lived in luxury, the French people stormed a fortress known as the Bastille. It was the beginning of the end. Louis was captured by his people and beheaded in 1793, sending shock waves throughout Europe. Suddenly, the young French Republic was fighting wars with just about every nearby country. In the ensuing chaos, a general named Napoleon Bonaparte (p. 45) came to rule France as emperor.

FEMALE PHARAOHS

∽ *Queens of the Nile* ∽

Ancient Egypt was no easy place to rule. Famines and floods routinely devastated the kingdom, and invading armies were always waiting at the borders to try to pluck power from the pharaoh's grasp. Some of Egypt's most successful leaders were women who had the brains and guts to rule one of history's most powerful civilizations.

Mistress of the Sky:
Ahmose-Nefertari (ca 1561–1494 B.C.)

Ahmose-Nefertari was born a princess of Thebes, a city in southern Egypt. But Egypt was at war with the Hyksos, a nomadic group from Asia that had conquered northern Egypt. Eventually, Nefertari's brother, Ahmose I, became pharaoh and successfully defeated the invaders. Male pharaohs often married their siblings, and Ahmose-Nefertari became the first queen of the New Kingdom, an era of prosperity for the civilization. When Ahmose I died, Ahmose-Nefertari kept her position of power, acting as regent for her young son Amenhotep. She was so widely beloved that after her death, she was deified, or made into a goddess. Known as the "Mistress of the Sky," she was worshipped as a resurrection goddess for the next 500 years. In statues and paintings, Ahmose-Nefertari is almost always depicted with black skin, a symbol of rebirth.

Beauty Queen:
Nefertiti (ca 1300s B.C.)

Nefertiti ruled alongside her husband, the pharaoh Akhenaten, and some historians believe she continued to rule on her own after her husband's death. Artwork from the time shows her as having more power than any female ruler before her—sometimes depicting her in roles normally reserved for male pharaohs, such as conquering enemies. Nefertiti and Akhenaten helped make Egypt wealthy and prosperous. They also set off one of its most tumultuous periods when they started a religion that, for a brief period, changed their culture from polytheism (the worship of many gods) to monotheism (the worship of one god). Today, Nefertiti is remembered by this painted sandstone bust, discovered in 1913, which made her an icon of beauty and power famous around the world.

The Last Pharaoh:
Cleopatra (69–30 B.C.)

Perhaps the most famous female pharaoh of all, Cleopatra VII was also the last pharaoh. She became queen at age 18 upon the death of her father and ruled with her two brothers and then her son. Intelligent, well educated, and fluent in six languages, she led Egypt for three decades. During a time when Egypt was under the threat of Roman rule, Cleopatra fought to keep her nation's independence—by using herself as a political playing piece. She charmed and married Roman commander Julius Caesar and then his successor, Mark Antony. With her access to their power—and their armies—she managed to bring wealth and success to Egypt in a precarious time. When she died, Egypt passed into the hands of Rome, ending the era of pharaohs.

The Queen Who Would Be King:
Hatshepsut (ca 1503–1458 B.C.)

She was the longest-reigning female pharaoh in Egypt—and one of the most successful rulers in her kingdom's history. She first ruled alongside her husband, Thutmose II. After his death, the crown went to Thutmose III, a son of one of the former pharaohs' secondary wives. But the king was too young to lead and Hatshepsut was declared regent. In her 20 years as pharaoh, she undertook huge building projects, including the temple at Deir el-Bahri, which is considered one of ancient Egypt's greatest architectural wonders. She authorized a trading expedition that brought back vast riches to her kingdom, including ivory, ebony, and gold. When she ruled, ancient Egypt had no words or images to describe a woman with Hatshepsut's status—so in paintings and reliefs, the pharaoh ordered herself depicted in a king's traditional garb, topped off with a fake beard and bulging muscles.

COMMANDING KINGS
Cleopatra's Contemporary
Julius Caesar (100–44 B.C.)

Julius Caesar was one of the most powerful generals of the ancient world. He conquered territory after territory, expanding Rome's control to the entire Mediterranean. Then, in 49 B.C., he returned from the battlefield and began waging a civil war against a faction of the Roman Senate. Caesar's fiercely loyal army prevailed, and the defeated Senate reluctantly declared Caesar *dictator perpetuo*—dictator for life. As dictator, Caesar spent a lot of effort trying to win over the common people: He opened private libraries to the public, extended citizenship to newly conquered peoples in Gaul (France), and even built shopping centers. But as much as the people loved Caesar, the Senate feared and hated him for turning their democracy into a dictatorship. So on March 15, 44 B.C., a group of senators famously ambushed and assassinated Caesar, putting an end to his reign.

ROYALS
WITH A
CAUSE
SOVEREIGNS
AND SOCIAL
ACTIVISTS

Rania of Jordan

∞ Queen of Progress ∞

Today she is a queen, but Rania of Jordan wasn't born a royal. From her birthplace in Kuwait, she and her family were forced to flee alongside hundreds of thousands of other Palestinians during the 1991 Gulf War. After earning a business degree, she took a job at Apple Inc. One night, she went to a dinner party with a co-worker and happened to meet Prince Abdullah II bin al-Hussein of Jordan. The commoner and the prince fell in love and married just five months later.

Rania's fairy-tale love story made her an instant international icon. Even though she never expected to spend her life in the limelight, Rania has embraced her new role and used her public position to help others. In the Arab world, where women are often prevented from having power and authority, Rania is a progressive female voice. She speaks out for women's rights and has helped found abuse counseling centers. She is also passionate about education: The mother of four believes every child has the right to modern classrooms, inspiring teachers, and current technology.

Rania also uses her position to help bridge the gap between the Middle East and the West. In March 2008, she created an online video series meant to show Western viewers what the Arab world is really like. Some have criticized her for talking about taboo topics in a public forum. But Rania believes that knowledge is the best way to solve social problems and bring cultures together. "The approach should be to talk about it, bring it to the surface," she says, "not to sweep it under the rug."

"We shouldn't judge people through the prism of our own stereotypes."
—Queen Rania

Royal Rundown

❋ **BORN:** August 31, 1970, Kuwait City, Kuwait
❋ **LEADS:** Jordan ❋ **KNOWN FOR:** Her work for social progress and cultural understanding

Catherine, Duchess of Cambridge

∽ Commoner to Queen ∽

Catherine—also called Kate—was born to airline employee parents whose fortunes changed in 1987. That's when they founded a mail-order party-goods company that became a surprise success. Kate and her younger sister and brother all attended exclusive boarding schools. Despite dealing with bullying, Kate excelled both in academics and athletics, captaining the school field hockey team.

In 2001, Kate went to the University of St. Andrews in Scotland to study art history. There she met and fell for a fellow student—Prince William of Wales, second in line to the throne and the future king of England. On April 29, 2011, the two were married at Westminster Abbey in one of the most publicized weddings in history. She became Catherine, Her Royal Highness the Duchess of Cambridge, and the future queen of England.

Catherine splits her time between raising her children and her many charity projects. Together with her husband and her brother-in-law Prince Harry, Kate founded the Royal Foundation of the Duke and Duchess of Cambridge and Prince Harry. Through the foundation, Catherine works with many charities, including one that helps care for children with life-threatening medical conditions, one that fights addiction, and another that advocates for mental health resources. This future queen is known for her adventurous spirit and love of children: She's taught kids how to light campfires, taken 150 children from one of her charities to see a play, and even donned boxing gloves and sparred a professional fighter to emphasize the role of physical exercise in mental health.

"I really hope I can make a difference, even in the smallest way."
—Catherine, Duchess of Cambridge

Royal Rundown

❀ **BORN:** January 9, 1982, Reading, England, U.K. ❀ **LEADS:** United Kingdom
❀ **KNOWN FOR:** Advocating for health and other modern issues through charitable work

RADICAL RULERS

Some wielded their power for good, enacting laws to protect their subjects. Others caused the downfall of their neighbors or even their own kingdoms. One thing is for sure: These queens all made their marks on history.

Viking, Saint, and Queen of Russia: Olga of Kiev (ca 890–969)

Today, Olga of Kiev is celebrated as a saint in both the Catholic and Eastern Orthodox Churches. But while she was alive, her behavior was far from saintly. Legends say Olga was born in modern-day northwest Russia to a family of Varyags—more commonly called Vikings. As far as historians know, her life was uneventful until her husband, Igor, Prince of Kiev, was murdered during a diplomatic mission by a nearby tribe called the Drevlians. Her son was too young to take the crown, so according to one legend, Olga stepped up in his stead and became queen. That gave the Drevlians an idea—to increase their power by having Olga marry their prince. When they sent a delegation of 20 men to propose the idea that Olga should unite with the very people who had killed her husband, she came up with a plan. She ordered the delegation destroyed. Then she told the Drevlian prince that she would marry him if he sent a party of tribesmen to accompany her on her journey. When he did, she had those men burned alive. But Olga wasn't done yet. She asked the prince—who still hadn't heard back from any of the men in the delegation—to prepare a funeral feast where they could all mourn her husband's death. At the feast, Olga ordered her soldiers to put the rest of the Drevlians to death. Finally satisfied, she went on to become the first ruler of the region to adopt Christianity—earning herself sainthood.

Righteous Ruler: Empress Theodora (ca 500–548)

Empress Theodora was truly a woman ahead of her time. Though she never ruled outright, she was the most trusted adviser of her husband, Emperor Justinian—and many historians think Theodora was actually the true leader. What's sure is that she was one of the most powerful women who ever lived in Byzantium, today called Istanbul, Turkey. The daughter of a commoner, Theodora grew up to be an actress, dancer, and comedian. At age 21, she met Justinian—a farmer's son who unexpectedly became emperor when his family rose to power. Because she had been a working-class woman herself, Theodora was familiar with their struggles. When she became empress, she used her newfound power to set up legislation that gave women new freedoms and protected them from abuse. Theodora was one of the first rulers in history to recognize women's rights.

First Queen of Her Kingdom: Seondeok of Silla (ca 606–647)

Blood was everything in the ancient kingdom of Silla, which ruled southeastern Korea for nearly 1,000 years after it was founded in 57 B.C. The strict "bone rank system" decreed that only members of the royal house of Kim, members of the sacred bone class, could rule. When King Jinpyeong died in 632 with no male heirs of the sacred bone rank, there was only one option for ruler: his daughter, Seondeok. When Seondeok took power, Silla was in constant battle with its neighboring nations for control of the Korean peninsula. Seondeok proved herself a skillful diplomat, sending envoys to broker deals with Silla's neighbors. And she wasn't afraid to send her armies into battle when she thought it necessary. Seondeok was even more successful in domestic affairs: She became known for encouraging a renaissance in arts and culture in her kingdom. She was so fascinated by astronomy that she ordered an observatory called the Tower of the Moon and Stars built in 632 in what today is Gyeongju, South Korea—now the oldest existing observatory in Asia. After Seondeok's reign, Silla continued to assert itself over the peninsula, which would eventually be unified under Silla for the first time.

Nation Breaker: Anne Boleyn (ca 1501–1536)

Though she was queen of England for only three years—her reign was cut short when her husband beheaded her—Anne Boleyn changed the course of the nation's history. Anne came to the court of King Henry VIII in 1522. Henry, who was already disenchanted with his wife, Queen Catherine of Aragon (p. 40), because she had not given birth to a male heir, fell head over heels—but Anne refused his attention. Henry was willing to do anything to marry Anne. He petitioned the pope to declare his marriage with Catherine illegitimate—but the pope refused. Breaking a centuries-old bond between the Catholic Church and the crown, Henry went behind the pope's back, had an archbishop annul the marriage, married Anne, and broke away from the Catholic Church by creating the new Church of England. After all that, Henry soon lost interest when Anne too failed to bear him a prince. He threw her in the Tower of London and had her beheaded on May 19, 1536—but not before Anne gave birth to a daughter, the future Elizabeth I (p. 12).

Queen for Nine Days vs. Queen for a Lifetime

Meet Great Britain's Shortest- and Longest-Serving Monarchs

Lady Jane Grey
(October 1537–February 12, 1554)

She's the shortest-reigning—and perhaps the most tragic—figure in the history of English royalty. Lady Jane Grey was used as a pawn on the chessboard of political power, but the game proved far too dangerous. She ruled for little more than a week before she lost her throne—and her head.

According to some accounts, Lady Jane was a petite, quiet, reserved teenager. But as the great-niece of Henry VIII, she was fourth in line for the crown after his son Edward VI and his daughters Mary (p. 40) and Elizabeth (p. 12). Jane's ambitious parents hoped to marry her to Edward, so they made sure she was well educated and a devout Protestant—the religion of the crown. But Edward was weak and sickly, and by 1553, it was clear that he wouldn't live much longer.

The Duke of Northumberland, John Dudley, ruled from behind the throne, and he knew that if Mary or Elizabeth took the crown, his days in power would be over. So he launched a plot to make his own family royal. He had the 15-year-old Jane marry his son against her will. Then the evil duke persuaded the dying Edward to declare his sisters illegitimate heirs and transfer the crown to Lady Jane instead. Edward died on July 6, and three days later Lady Jane was informed that she was the queen. After fainting, she reluctantly accepted. But Mary, with the support of the people, claimed that the throne rightfully belonged to her. Jane—who had never wanted the job anyway—was relieved, but that didn't last long. She was arrested and imprisoned in the Tower of London. Considered too big of a threat to the rightful ruler to live, she was executed on February 12, 1554, at age 16.

Elizabeth II

(April 21, 1926–)

Crowned on June 2, 1953, Queen Elizabeth II of Great Britain is the longest-reigning monarch in British history. In February 2017, she celebrated her Sapphire Jubilee—65 years on the throne.

When Elizabeth was born, nobody realized that she would someday be queen. She was the daughter of the second son of the monarchs King George V and Queen Mary. Elizabeth was educated at home by tutors in French, math, history, dancing, singing, and art. In 1936, her quiet life was turned upside down when her grandfather George V died, making her uncle Edward the new king. But Edward was in love with American socialite Wallis Simpson. He had to choose between the crown and marrying Simpson, who was divorced—and he chose to marry. When Edward abdicated the throne, Elizabeth's father became king, making Elizabeth princess and heir.

Elizabeth began training for her royal role. She made public appearances and official visits. When World War II broke out, the 14-year-old princess famously made radio broadcasts reassuring the people. In 1945, she trained side by side with ordinary British citizens to be a driver and mechanic in the war effort. In 1947, she married her longtime love, Philip Mountbatten, collecting clothing coupons to get enough fabric for her gown during post-wartime rationing. She quickly had two children, Charles and Anne. On February 6, 1952, her father died, and Elizabeth became the ruling monarch. For the first time in history, the coronation was broadcast on television.

Over her long reign, Elizabeth has guided England through major constitutional changes, wars, and conflicts. As a constitutional monarch, Elizabeth has no political powers, but she is careful to keep the tradition of the crown alive. Popular with her people, she's a beloved queen who has led the monarchy into the modern age.

Marie Antoinette

When Marie Antoinette ascended the throne of France at just 18 years old, she took charge of a country that was teetering on the brink of revolution. At first, her people loved the beautiful, frivolous queen, who lived in the gold-plated, velvet-draped Palace of Versailles and ordered 300 new dresses each year. But soon they turned against her: Marie Antoinette became a symbol of the monarchy's excess while her people suffered, and the people revolted, ending her reign.

EXPENSIVE TASTES

In May 1770, 14-year-old Marie Antoinette traveled from her birthplace in Vienna, Austria, to France to meet her husband-to-be, the future king Louis XVI of France. Her entourage included 57 carriages, 117 footmen, and 376 horses. With her gray-blue eyes and ash blond hair, Marie was known as a delicate beauty. The people of France loved her at first sight—but she didn't impress Louis. Introverted and shy, he was a poor match for his outgoing, outspoken queen.

Bored with her husband, Marie Antoinette found entertainment elsewhere. She filled the court with a clever, vivacious circle and spent most of her time socializing. She dressed in the latest trends and became France's fashion icon. But Marie began to take things too far. She spared no cost in indulging her extravagant tastes—often spending twice her annual clothing budget of about $3.6 million in today's money. Once, she ordered a model farm to be built on the palace grounds so that she and her ladies-in-waiting could dress up in costumes and pretend to be milkmaids and shepherdesses.

There's no evidence that Marie Antoinette ever said "Let them eat cake" in reference to France's starving peasants.

Marie Antoinette was a lover of music. She was also a musician herself. In this painting, made during her lifetime, she is shown playing her favorite instrument: the harp.

REBELLION AND REVOLT

The French people began to grow resentful of the royal family's spending, and Marie was the perfect person on whom to hang their frustrations. It became fashionable to blame the young queen for all France's problems. And the people had a lot to complain about: A bad harvest had made the price of grain skyrocket, causing them to go hungry. Mobs began to riot in the street, demanding bread to eat.

But in the glittering palace of Versailles, Marie and Louis were totally out of touch with their subjects' plight. The queen continued to spend a fortune building and furnishing her private residence at Versailles, the Petit Trianon; the total cost was about six million dollars in today's money.

But the difficulties facing France were not entirely Marie's fault. The wars of the 18th century—especially the American Revolution, in which France backed the colonists—had put France in massive debt. And while ordinary people were squeezed by high taxes, the upper classes didn't have to pay them at all. King Louis and his advisers tried to institute a fairer tax system, but the upper class resisted. As conditions worsened for the French people, many blamed the royals, and Marie was their main target. On July 14, 1789, 900 French workers and peasants stormed the Bastille prison to arm themselves with guns and ammunition. The French Revolution had begun.

Royal Rundown

❀ **BORN:** November 2, 1755, Vienna, Austria
❀ **DIED:** October 16, 1793, Paris, France
❀ **LED:** France ❀ **REMEMBERED FOR:**
Symbolizing the fall of the French monarchy

END OF AN ERA

King Louis was paralyzed by fear, so Marie stepped into his place, meeting with advisers and writing letters to other Europeans royals begging for help in saving France's monarchy. She plotted the royal family's escape in June 1791, but they were captured. The monarchy was abolished, and Marie and Louis were arrested, dragged to the guillotine, and executed in 1793. Marie Antoinette, the last queen of France, became a symbol of a monarchy that fell in the face of revolution.

Mothers of the Revolution:
The Women's March on Versailles

Women have begun social and political movements throughout history, including protests against unjust rulers. On the morning of October 5, 1789, women in a Paris market became furious when there was no bread to buy for their families. They began moving through the city, demanding food at a fair price, and their ranks swelled as more women joined the cause. After six hours of marching in the pouring rain, a crowd of thousands of armed and angry civilians arrived at the source of the problem: the Palace of Versailles, where Louis XVI and Marie Antoinette were cowering in fear. The pressure of the protesters forced the royals out of Versailles and into Paris, an early turning point in what would become the French Revolution.

FEMALE FIRSTS
IN U.S. GOVERNMENT

∾ *Leading American Women* ∾

These women had to fight every step of the way to get to their groundbreaking roles in the United States government. In doing so, they not only changed history, they also paved the way for the next generation of justices and congresswomen.

Ceiling Shatterer:
Madeleine Albright (1937–)

As a toddler, Madeleine Albright fled with her family from Prague, Czechoslovakia, as Hitler invaded the city in 1939. They later returned, only to flee for their lives again when the Communists came to power in 1948. They settled in Denver, Colorado, U.S.A., where Albright excelled at school, especially in debate and international affairs. After graduating from Wellesley College, in Massachusetts, in 1959, she continued to study Russian and international relations while raising her three daughters. Eventually, she earned a Ph.D. and learned seven languages. In 1993, she was named U.S. ambassador to the United Nations. Four years later, she became the first female secretary of state. She advocated for supporting human rights and democracy throughout the world and halting the spread of nuclear weapons. In 2012, President Barack Obama awarded her the highest honor a U.S. civilian can earn—the Presidential Medal of Freedom.

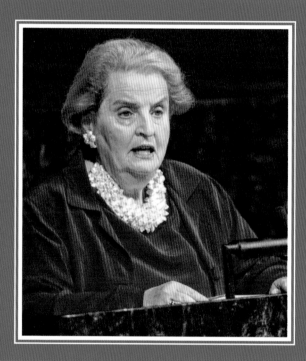

Boundary Breaker:
Tammy Baldwin (1962–)

Tammy Baldwin is known for her focus on energy issues, universal health care, and LGBTQ (lesbian, gay, bisexual, transgender, and queer) rights—the last a cause close to her heart, as she was the first openly gay politician elected to the U.S. Senate. Born in Madison, Wisconsin, Baldwin graduated first in her high school class and went on to major in mathematics and government, then attain a law degree in 1989. While practicing law, she worked her way up Wisconsin's political ladder, then became a U.S. representative, and, in 2012, made history when she was elected to the U.S. Senate. She has helped pass legislation that supports marriage equality and equal rights and has advocated for government-supported health care for all. Though she was told repeatedly that her youth, gender, and sexual orientation would prevent people from voting for her, she's proved her critics wrong. "The key to success in any endeavor is to ignore the naysayers and the cynics and go for it with all you've got," she says.

Limit Pusher:
Sonia Sotomayor (1954–)

When President Barack Obama nominated Sonia Sotomayor to the Supreme Court in 2009, she became the first Latina in U.S. history to serve on the high court. Born in 1954 in the South Bronx area of New York City, she's the child of a nurse mother and a machine worker father. When Sotomayor's father died in 1963, her mother worked hard to provide her children a good education on a meager budget, pushing them to become fluent in English and making sacrifices to buy them a set of encyclopedias. After earning a law degree from Yale Law School, in 1979, Sotomayor did pro bono work that caught the attention of several senators. They helped appoint her as a U.S. district court judge in 1992. As a Supreme Court justice, Sotomayor has helped make landmark rulings, including *Obergefell* v. *Hodges*, which made same-sex marriage legal in all 50 states.

Status Shaker:
Jeannette Rankin (1880–1973)

Jeannette Rankin was a suffragette who in 1919 helped pass the 19th Amendment to the U.S. Constitution, giving women the right to vote. Just a few years prior, she had pushed women's rights to the next level when she became the first woman to serve in the U.S. Congress. Rankin was one of seven children born to a rancher and schoolteacher in Missoula, Montana. As a student at the University of Washington in Seattle, she discovered the women's rights movement and found her calling. She helped the suffragettes campaign to get women the vote, and her efforts helped her home state of Montana pass the effort into law in 1914. In 1916, Rankin ran a neck-and-neck race for the U.S. House of Representatives and won, becoming the first woman to serve in Congress. "I may be the first woman member of Congress," she famously said when she won, "but I won't be the last."

COMMANDING KINGS **Congressman for Change**
John Lewis (1940–)

While growing up in the Deep South, where black people were terrorized for not "knowing their place," young John Lewis was warned by his parents to stay out of trouble. He didn't listen. Lewis got into what he calls "necessary trouble" after seeing the success of the Montgomery bus boycotts, in which African Americans in Montgomery, Alabama, refused to ride city buses in protest against segregated seating. Authorities in the South resorted to all sorts of dirty tactics to try to keep black people from voting, including literacy tests, poll taxes, and complicated voter registration systems. On March 7, 1965, Lewis and hundreds of other protesters were beaten by police while leading a march for voting rights across the Edmund Pettus Bridge near Selma, Alabama. News footage showing the unprovoked police brutality of "Bloody Sunday" helped speed up the passage of the Voting Rights Act of 1965. Lewis continued to push for voting rights and was elected to the House of Representatives in 1986. Today, he is one of the most respected members of Congress for his dedication to protecting the civil rights of all Americans.

Nwanyeruwa

∾ Fighting for Fairness ∾

Many think Nwanyeruwa's "Women's War" was the first major challenge to British authority in colonial West Africa.

For many generations, gender roles in Nigerian society were balanced. Women participated in government meetings, sold their own goods in markets, and worked side by side with men on domestic tasks. Women also collaborated with each other in powerful networks to influence political decisions. That all changed in 1914, when British colonists took over Nigeria.

The British paid little attention to the traditional power structure. Instead, they decided to control Nigeria through representatives called warrant chiefs. Over time, the warrant chiefs began to abuse their power. They confiscated women's animals and the money they made from market sales. The warrant chiefs forced women to marry them against their will. Then, in 1925, the British government conducted a census of all the Nigerian people's possessions and placed a tax on them. At first, only the men were taxed, but even as the world entered a massive economic depression in 1929, rumors began circulating that soon the women would have to start paying as well.

Though not much is known about her, in October 1929, a woman known as Nwanyeruwa was reportedly approached by a census taker who commanded her to count up her animals and family members. Nwanyeruwa went to tell the women in her network what had happened. Within a few weeks, thousands of women had gathered outside their local government office, demanding written assurance that they would not be taxed. After several days of waiting in peaceful protest, their demands were met. When women across Nigeria heard about what had happened, they started organizing, creating a protest that spanned 6,000 square miles (15,540 sq km). This "Women's War" forced the British to replace their system with a more fair one—and it all started with Nwanyeruwa.

Royal Rundown

BORN: unknown, Nigeria   **DIED:** ca 1900s, Nigeria   **LED:** Nigeria
REMEMBERED FOR: Protecting women's rights by beginning Nigeria's Women's War

Tawakkol Karman

∽ Fighting for Freedom ∽

I n a country where most women are neither seen nor heard, it seems unlikely that a 32-year-old mother of three would come along to head a revolution. But that's the story of Tawakkol Karman, a journalist who leads nonviolent protests to support women's rights and democratic freedom.

Karman grew up in tumultuous times. She watched as North and South Yemen first united in 1990, then battled each other in civil war in 1994. When the North won, its repressive government took control of the country. The new leadership was corrupt and unjust, falsely accusing journalists, committing war crimes against its citizens, and not treating women as equals.

Along with several colleagues, Karman founded Women Journalists Without Chains in 2005 to support freedom of the press. Starting in 2007, she began protesting in the nation's capital every Tuesday, a practice she has continued for many years—even though she has been arrested several times. Though her protests are peaceful, the political atmosphere of Yemen means they put her in great danger. In 2010, she narrowly escaped when a would-be assassin tried to stab her.

In 2011, a movement called the Arab Spring swept across the Middle East. Civilians protested against unfair governments and human rights violations. Karman led her protesters to support the movement and ended up in jail. Furious, her people came out in mass demonstrations against the Yemeni president 'Alī 'Abd Allāh Sālih. When Karman was freed the next day, she went right back to the protest. For her brave leadership, Karman was awarded the Nobel Peace Prize in October 2011. She is the first Arab woman and one of the youngest people ever to win. Karman donated the $500,000 prize to help victims of the Arab Spring uprising.

> "Peace does not mean just to stop wars, but also to stop oppression and injustice."
> —Tawakkol Karman

Royal Rundown

❀ **BORN:** February 7, 1979, Taiz, Yemen ❀ **LEADS:** Yemen ❀ **KNOWN FOR:** Fighting for the rights of a free press and fair government

Power Tools

FIT FOR A Queen

Today, a woman in a leadership position is often still seen as revolutionary. But as far back as 5,000 years ago, ancient Egypt was ruled by female pharaohs who were just as mighty as their male contemporaries. In that culture, pharaohs were often depicted holding a crook, a flail, and other symbols of power that were destined to stick around.

The Headdress

Pharaohs are often depicted wearing a cloth headpiece, called a *nemes*. None of these crown-like coverings have ever been discovered, leading experts to believe they may have been used only in artistic depictions of the pharaoh, to show how important he—or she—was.

The Crook

Known as the *heka* in Egyptian, the crook originated from the staff carried by shepherds: a long, sturdy stick with a hook at one end they used to guide their sheep. The crook represented the responsibility of the pharaoh to lead the people of Egypt.

The Flail

Known as the *nekhakha* in Egyptian, the flail was made up of a handle with three beaded strands attached to the top. Some historians think shepherds used the flail to defend their animals, and that it symbolized the pharaoh's role of punishing evildoers. Others think the flail was a farming tool used for harvesting grain. They say the flail represented the pharaoh's task of protecting the land and ensuring that the people had enough to eat.

Throne Clone

In 2016, experts at Harvard University re-created the throne of an ancient Egyptian queen named Hetepheres. Hetepheres, the mother of the pharaoh Khufu, who built the Great Pyramid at Giza, sat upon this royal chair around 2600 B.C. Relying on a mixed-up puzzle of tiny fragments and old records from the 1925 discovery of Hetepheres's tomb, the experts reconstructed how the throne used to look. Made of cedar wood, bright blue tiles, gold foil, and copper, it was truly a chair fit for a queen.

Sovereign Symbol

Ancient Egyptian leaders haven't been the only kings and queens to use a staff to represent their power. Many have wielded something similar. Perhaps the most famous example is the Royal Scepter, which a new British monarch holds in her right hand as the crown of England is placed upon her head for the first time.

Dressed as a King

During the first six years of her reign, the pharaoh Hatshepsut, a woman who ruled from 1507 to 1458 B.C., was usually depicted as slim, graceful, and female. But for the rest of her rule, Hatshepsut decided to change her image. From then on, she always appeared as a man, with a broad chest, a beard, and powerful muscles.

This statue depicting Queen Hatshepsut as the god of Osiris sits on her mortuary temple, Deir el-Bahri, in Thebes, Egypt. Ancient Egyptians believed their pharaohs became Osiris after death.

CULTURE SHAPERS

Not every queen wears a crown. The women in this chapter aren't real-life royals, but they are remarkable leaders all the same. They've dominated many different fields—including acting, athletics, journalism, fashion—and each has risen to the top of her trade. They led people, movements, and new industries. They are pioneering women who changed culture forever. And, well, they just plain rule.

Mary Tyler Moore

❧ Monarch of the Modern Woman ❧

Mary Tyler Moore is most famous for playing Mary Richards, a working woman who was independent, over 30, single, and more interested in her career than marriage. That might not sound all that earth-shattering now, but in 1970, when *The Mary Tyler Moore Show* was launched, it most definitely was. Mary Richards's determination and spunk were an inspiration to American women who were making their own way in a world that wasn't quite ready for them.

BREAKING IN

Mary Tyler Moore's family moved from New York to Los Angeles when she was eight years old. Moore acted and danced in high school and, in the mid-1950s, got her first professional acting job playing a dancing elf in a commercial for home appliances. She got her big break in 1961, when she landed the role of television wife Laura Petrie in *The Dick Van Dyke Show*. Moore won two Emmys for her work on the show as a stay-at-home mom who famously appeared in capri pants instead of dresses, a revolutionary choice at the time.

After *The Dick Van Dyke Show* ended in 1966, Moore decided it was time for her to take the lead and create her own character. Along with her husband, Grant Tinker, she formed her own company—MTM Enterprises—and pitched a show to CBS about a recently divorced woman making it on her own. CBS liked the idea, but it didn't like the subject of divorce, which was at the time a taboo topic on network television. With the compromise that new

"Take chances, make mistakes. That's how you grow. Pain nourishes your courage. You have to fail in order to practice being brave."
—*Mary Tyler Moore*

Royal Rundown

❀ **BORN:** December 29, 1936, New York, New York, U.S.A. ❀ **DIED:** January 25, 2017, Greenwich, Connecticut, U.S.A.
❀ **LED:** TV sitcoms of the 1960s and '70s ❀ **REMEMBERED FOR:** A body of work that inspired a generation

character Mary Richards would be newly single instead of newly divorced, the show launched.

BECOMING AN ICON

Mary Richards was an associate news producer at a Minneapolis television station. She spent her days juggling the egos of her male co-workers and her nights commiserating with her friends and neighbors. Richards was one of the first television characters who was a successful single woman, and the show became a cultural sensation.

At a time when America's attitudes about women with careers were shifting, a lot of real-life working women looked up to Mary Richards—who faced her challenges with courage and humor—as a model to help them find their place in the workforce. And the character inspired nearly all the female sitcom stars that would follow in her footsteps, from Jennifer Aniston to Tina Fey.

LEAVING A LEGACY

Moore won three Emmy Awards for her role as Richards, and her production company grew to produce many other era-defining television programs, such as sitcoms *Taxi* and *Cheers*, as well as the police drama *Hill Street Blues*, which was nominated for a whopping 98 Emmy Awards. When *The Mary Tyler Moore Show* ended in 1977, Moore set out to prove that she was more than the smiling, plucky Mary Richards. She played more serious roles in acclaimed plays and films like *Ordinary People*, about a family struggling with the loss of a teenage son.

Moore's personal life was shadowed with tragedy: divorce, health struggles, and the death of her only child. But she used her fame to raise awareness for Type 1 diabetes, a condition she dealt with from her diagnosis at age 33 until the end of her life. When Moore died at the age of 80, the world mourned the loss of a woman who led the way for others into a new era—on television and in real life, too.

Moore and her fellow winners from *The Dick Van Dyke Show* pose with their statuettes at the 16th Annual Primetime Emmy Awards on May 25, 1964 (left). Moore with her castmates on *The Mary Tyler Moore Show* (above).

COMMANDING KINGS

The New Faces of Television

Norman Lear (1922–)

He's sometimes nicknamed "King" Lear for the role he's played in shaping modern television. Norman Lear's reign began in 1971, when the screenwriter and producer began work on a new show called *All in the Family*. The comedy followed the foibles of narrow-minded Archie Bunker as he navigated—usually not very well—a society that was changing around him. The show bravely took on topics that were considered television taboo at the time, such as race, inequality, and social injustice. Lear didn't stop there. He tackled women's rights with his show *Maude* and brought black actors into starring roles, including Sherman Hemsley and Isabel Sanford as the title characters in *The Jeffersons*. When criticized for airing his political opinions, Lear responded, "Why wouldn't I have ideas and thoughts, and why wouldn't my work reflect those ideas?"

NEWS QUEENS

❧ *Front-Page Females* ❧

Journalism used to be seen as too rough, too competitive, and too brainy for women. To break into the field, female journalists had to be smarter, tougher, and braver than their competitors. These royals of the news didn't just conquer the industry; they came to lead it.

Master of the Interview:
Barbara Walters (1929–)

Barbara Walters has probably interviewed more powerful people than anyone else in TV history. She started out writing for television and eventually worked her way up to co-host of the NBC show *Today* in 1964. But she wasn't treated with the respect her position deserved: She was called "the Today girl" rather than her actual title of co-host. And when an especially powerful person came on the show, Walters had to wait to speak until the fourth question, deferring to her male co-host. Undaunted, Walters focused on honing her interviewing technique. In 1975, she won her first Emmy, for best host in a talk series. In 1976, Walters accepted a job—and an unprecedented one-million-dollar salary—as the first female co-anchor of a network evening news show. In her decades on the air, she has interviewed actors, athletes, foreign leaders, and every U.S. president since Richard Nixon.

News Breaker, News Maker:
Soledad O'Brien (1966–)

When Soledad O'Brien's parents, an interracial couple, were first married in 1958, they couldn't sit at the same table at restaurants and people spit on them in the street. So O'Brien made it her mission to give a voice to those who society doesn't listen to. In doing so, she's become one of television news' most prominent voices herself. After studying at Harvard University, O'Brien became the co-anchor of CNN's morning program, where she broke news stories on Hurricane Katrina and the London terrorist attacks in July 2005. Today, she anchors her own show, *Matter of Fact With Soledad O'Brien*, and makes critically acclaimed documentaries on the world's top issues, including race and prejudice. She has received numerous awards for her exhaustive reporting and insightful coverage.

Female at the Front:
Christiane Amanpour (1958–)

In 2002, *Vanity Fair* magazine called her "the world's most famous war reporter." In her 30 years as a journalist, Christiane Amanpour has covered some of the world's deadliest conflicts—and she has never let danger keep her from getting the story. Born in 1958 in London to an English mother and Iranian father, Amanpour spent part of her childhood in Iran, until 1979, when the country underwent a revolution. She studied journalism and got a job at CNN in 1983. At first, the channel didn't want to put her on the air because with her dark hair and foreign accent, she was different from other American anchors at the time—but when she started winning awards and acclaim for her coverage of conflicts in Iran and Bosnia, she gained respect. Eventually, she became CNN's chief international journalist. Amanpour has earned every major television journalism award for her fearless reporting in war-torn nations worldwide.

Pioneer of the Pen:
Gwen Ifill (1955–2016)

Starting at age nine, Gwen Ifill knew that she wanted to be a journalist. The daughter of Caribbean immigrants, she grew up in the 1960s, a time when racial tensions were at a breaking point in the United States. "I didn't see a whole lot of people who looked like me doing it on television," she said, but "you get used to being underestimated." After graduating college in 1977, Ifill went to work for a series of prestigious newspapers, including the *Washington Post* and the *New York Times*. In 1994, she switched to television news, where her journalistic skills caught the eye of PBS, which hired her as a correspondent. In 2004, Ifill was the first African-American woman to moderate a vice presidential debate, and, in 2013, she and journalist Judy Woodruff became the first female duo ever to co-anchor a network news program, the PBS *NewsHour*. For her pioneering journalism, she was awarded dozens of accolades, including a prestigious Peabody Award, and more than 20 honorary doctorates from universities around the world.

COMMANDING KINGS
From the Front Lines
Ernie Pyle (1900–1945)

When American soldiers charged the battlefields from Africa to Okinawa in World War II, a slight, middle-aged man named Ernie Pyle followed close behind, wielding a pen and notepad instead of a rifle. As one of the first "embedded journalists," Pyle lived among the troops he covered and shared their dangers. He became one of the war's most popular correspondents, famous for a reporting style that showed the terror of combat and the situation of soldiers mired in muddy foxholes. Pyle's stories earned him a Pulitzer Prize, and his death to Japanese machine-gun fire near the end of the war brought tears to the eyes of millions of readers. The job of war correspondent is no less dangerous today: Reporters covering conflicts around the globe put their lives on the line to tell the stories of war.

Kay Koplovitz

❧ Sovereign of Satellite ❧

n 1966, Kay Koplovitz was a college student backpacking through London when she saw an advertisement for a lecture on satellite communication. Though the term was meaningless to her—at the time, there were no cell phones, no internet, and no cable channels—Koplovitz was intrigued. In the lecture, she learned that three satellites orbiting the Earth had the potential to broadcast anything all over the world simultaneously. The idea would change her life.

Koplovitz dropped her pre-med major and focused instead on learning everything she could about satellite technology and the television business. Seven years later, when opportunity came her way, she was ready. She pioneered the first ever live sporting event broadcast via satellite: a championship boxing match between Muhammad Ali and Joe Frazier. The event changed the course of television history, proving that satellite broadcasting was the future. In 1977, Koplovitz launched a new network called USA and became the first woman to head a television network. She led USA to become the number one most-watched primetime network. After dominating the TV industry, Koplovitz went on to found an organization called Springboard Enterprises, which has helped female entrepreneurs launch companies like Zipcar and iRobot.

Along the way, Koplovitz has faced plenty of challenges as a woman in a field dominated by men. When she was getting started, the only women in the television business were working as secretaries. She often wasn't taken seriously. Sometimes, she wasn't even allowed to do her job—like when she was refused entry to TV events held at the men-only Augusta National Golf Club, in Georgia. But Koplovitz didn't let that stop her. "I was never thinking that it was going to be a barrier for me," she said. "I was going to find a way around it because I knew if I was to be successful I would have to."

> "This is what I want for entrepreneurs, especially for women: to believe in themselves, to dream bigger, reach higher, and to achieve success beyond their wildest expectations."
> —Kay Koplovitz

Royal Rundown

❀ **BORN:** April 11, 1945, Milwaukee, Wisconsin, U.S.A. ❀ **LEADS:** The USA television network ❀ **KNOWN FOR:** Becoming the first woman in history to serve as president of a TV network

Oprah Winfrey

∽ Queen of Media ∽

Today, Oprah Winfrey is worth more than three billion dollars and has been called the most influential woman in the world. But she had to fight her way to the top. Winfrey was born in a rural Mississippi town in 1954, when schools, bathrooms, water fountains, and public transportation were still segregated. She grew up in extreme poverty, sometimes wearing potato sacks to school because her mother couldn't afford clothes.

At age 14, Winfrey went to live with her father in Nashville, Tennessee. She studied hard, became an honor roll student at her high school, and took an after-school job working for a local black radio station, where she discovered her passion for media. In 1973, she became Nashville's first African-American TV correspondent and the youngest news co-anchor ever at station WTVF. When she was fired less than eight months after starting because her producers thought she got too emotional on air, she didn't let the setback keep her down. She scored a job at *A.M. Chicago,* the lowest-rated talk show in Chicago, Illinois. Within a month, she had turned it into the highest-rated talk show. Three years later, it was renamed *The Oprah Winfrey Show.*

Winfrey became beloved by audiences everywhere for her warm personality and her fearlessness in tackling issues facing American women. Her show aired for 25 seasons, from 1986 to 2011, making it one of the longest-running daytime shows of all time. Winfrey went on to produce popular spin-off shows like *Rachael Ray,* found her own magazine, start a radio channel and a cable channel, and give millions of dollars to charity. She is considered one of the most prominent voices in modern American culture.

"Challenges are gifts that force us to search for a new center of gravity. Don't fight them. Just find a new way to stand."
—*Oprah Winfrey*

Royal Rundown

BORN: January 29, 1954, Kosciusko, Mississippi, U.S.A.
LEADS: Media   **KNOWN FOR:** A media empire

QUEENS
OF THE PEN

∽ *Royals of Children's Literature* ∾

Once upon a time, the only children's books around were meant to teach kids to read. Today, bookshelves are bursting with stories about kids finding adventure, discovering their voices, and navigating the sometimes treacherous terrain on the road to adulthood. It never would have happened if not for these queens of the pen.

Monarch of Magic:
J.K. Rowling (1965–)

J.K. Rowling is beloved worldwide as the creator of the Harry Potter books, which have sold so many copies that if you lined them all up end to end, they would circle the planet six times. But J.K. Rowling's life wasn't always magical. In 1994, she was a 28-year-old single mother relying on welfare and living in a cramped apartment in Edinburgh, Scotland, with her infant daughter. All she had was a dream: Four years previously, she had been sitting on a delayed train when the idea for a young boy who finds out he's a wizard came to her. She spent five years outlining a seven-book series, then began writing in cafés every spare second she got, her young daughter sleeping in a stroller next to her. In 1999, Rowling became an international sensation when the first three Harry Potter books took the top three slots in the *New York Times* best-seller list. The books became a publishing phenomenon, with millions of kids in round glasses and wizard's robes eagerly awaiting the midnight release of each new installment.

Children's Champion:
Judy Blume (1938–)

Judy Blume has been making up stories since childhood. She thought up tales when she was bouncing a ball, playing with paper dolls, and practicing the piano. But she never thought she could be a writer—until her children started school and Blume finally tried to take one of the stories in her head and put it down on paper. In the early 1970s, the honest way Blume approached usually taboo topics like puberty (*Are You There God? It's Me, Margaret*), racism (*Iggie's House*), bullying (*Blubber*), and divorce (*It's Not the End of the World*) struck a chord with adolescent girls everywhere. But it made some people upset, and many school libraries banned her books. That led Blume to become an activist who speaks out against censorship. She went on to pen 29 titles in total, which have sold more than 80 million copies in 31 languages. Bloom still gets 1,000 letters and emails a month from fans.

Adventure Writer:
E. L. Konigsburg (1930–2013)

E. L. Konigsburg taught high school science before she began writing children's books. She thought that, just like teaching, writing children's books was a way to share knowledge and wisdom with the next generation. She's known for books that transport her readers to unusual places and introduce them to unusual people, like her 1967 classic *From the Mixed-Up Files of Mrs. Basil E. Frankweiler*, a story about two kids who run away from home to the Metropolitan Museum of Art in New York City and find themselves in a mystery. The book won the American Library Association's John Newbery Medal, the nation's highest award for children's literature. The very same year, her book *Jennifer, Hecate, Macbeth, William McKinley, and Me, Elizabeth* won a Newbery Honor. She is the only author ever to win the Newbery Medal and a Newbery Honor in the same year. But the awards didn't stop there. With her 1996 book *The View from Saturday*, she won the top award again, becoming one of a handful of authors who have won the Newbery Medal twice.

Born Storyteller:
Mildred D. Taylor (1943–)

When she was a child, Mildred D. Taylor and her family made frequent trips from their home in Toledo, Ohio, U.S.A., back to her birthplace, Jackson, Mississippi. There, her family would trade tales about the struggles of friends and relatives growing up in the South, such as Taylor's great-grandfather—the son of a slave woman and a white plantation owner—who'd run away to make a life for himself in the North. After graduating from high school, Taylor began writing novels based on the family histories she grew up hearing. Her 1976 book, *Roll of Thunder, Hear My Cry*, received the Newbery Medal, and she went on to write one acclaimed novel after another. Some have criticized her books for using racially charged language, but Taylor stands up for her work, saying that it speaks the truth about a painful past that today's kids deserve to know about.

Noble Novelist:
Katherine Paterson (1932–)

Katherine Paterson was born the middle child of five kids in Qingjiang, China. Her parents were missionaries, and the family moved 18 times before Paterson's 18th birthday. By the time they finally settled in North Carolina, U.S.A., in 1940, Paterson had a British accent and wore unfamiliar clothes that made her an outcast. Many of her most famous characters are outcasts, too: Her best known book, *Bridge to Terabithia*, is about a newcomer to the fifth grade and a life-changing friendship she makes with a boy who really needs a friend. Many of Paterson's other books deal with the themes of pain and tragedy, but they've become beloved by generations because they help kids explore their feelings about tough topics. Her books have won many awards (including two Newbery Medals, just like Konigsburg), and two have been made into feature films.

Queens of Fashion

Throughout history, fashion trends have often dictated that women sacrifice comfort in the name of staying stylish: corsets squeeze, pencil skirts constrict, high heels pinch. But a few bold innovators have stood out, introducing fashions created for comfort, practicality, and power. These daring designers created the newest styles and empowered women while doing it. They are true queens of fashion.

1910s: Mary Phelps Jacob

Women have been binding and lifting their chests since at least the time of ancient Greece, when they would wrap strips of fabric around themselves and tie them in the back. Fast-forward to the 1500s, when women wore even more confining corsets made of whalebone to give their waists a nipped-in look. Five hundred years later, a new fashion trend emerged that didn't jibe with the traditional undergarment: sleek, slim dresses that would show every lump and bump. While dressing for a New York City ball in 1913, 19-year-old socialite Mary Phelps Jacob (also known as Caresse Crosby) became frustrated when her corset kept peeking out of her dress. So she asked her maid to bring her two pocket handkerchiefs and some pink ribbon, sewed them together, and the bra was born. Jacob's invention gave her a new freedom of movement that was the envy of her social circle. She filed for a patent on her design in 1914, and once her creation caught on, women everywhere shoved their corsets in the closet and never looked back.

1920s: Coco Chanel

No designer is more iconic than Coco Chanel. Starting in the 1920s, she freed women from restricting, heavy clothing once and for all. During World War II, women traded in their skirts for pants when they took over traditionally male jobs, such as manufacturing plane parts, to help the war effort while the men were busy fighting. But Chanel pioneered pants as a fashion statement, and stylish women followed suit. She was the first designer to use jersey, a comfortable, practical fabric previously reserved for men's underwear. She came up with the little black dress, which quickly became the staple of many women's wardrobes. And she borrowed from menswear when she created her iconic suits with boxy, collarless jackets—creating the perfect choice for postwar women bravely stepping into the male-dominated workplace for the first time. With these innovations, she was the first designer to see women as more than decorative objects—creating a wardrobe that they could conquer the world in.

1970s: Diane von Fürstenberg

Diane von Fürstenberg isn't just fashion royalty—she's a real-life royal! As a college student on vacation, the Belgium-born Diane Simone Michelle Halfin met Austro-Italian Prince Egon von Fürstenberg, heir to the Fiat automobile fortune. The couple fell in love and got married, but von Fürstenberg wanted to make her own way in the world. So she did. She learned how to make and manufacture clothing, and in the mid-1970s, she got her big break. That's when she released her iconic wrap dress. Its cut flattered just about any shape, and its silk jersey fabric traveled well, never wrinkled, and was affordable. Its versatile style made it both professional business attire and an elegant dinner dress. In an era where women felt pressured to dress like men—in unflattering suits—for career success, it showed women that they could be professional and express their own style all at once. It was instantly popular. By 1975, von Fürstenberg was making 15,000 dresses a week, and everyone from suburban housewives to First Lady Betty Ford wore them.

1980s: Donna Karan

In the 1980s, women went from being telephone operators and secretaries to competing with men in the race up the career ladder. But they didn't have the wardrobe to reflect their newfound role. Their workwear styles were borrowed from the boys: jackets, bow ties, and button-downs. But women didn't want to copy men; they wanted to stand out from them. Enter Donna Karan. She created the first capsule wardrobe, called "Seven Easy Pieces," a set of clothing that women could mix and match to create work outfits with minimum fuss. For the first time, women had a business wardrobe that was professional—but made them look like women. It was a fashion revelation that helped women make their place in the modern world.

2000s: Rei Kawakubo

For far too long, women wore clothing with men in mind: first, to appeal to their idea of what a woman should look like and, later, to fit in with them in the workplace. But forward-thinking Japanese designer Rei Kawakubo dresses women to please only themselves. Her designs are wearable works of art. With their oversize geometric shapes, shredded hems, and lots of bright colors, her clothes aren't the most wearable. And they're not exactly beautiful, either. But that's not the point: Kawakubo wants her designs to spark an emotional response. Kawakubo worked in the advertising department at a textile company before she started designing her own clothes in 1968, under the fashion label Comme des Garçons. Her designs were so shockingly different that by the time she debuted her line in Paris, in 1981, Kawakubo already had legions of dedicated fans. Today, the fashion label earns more than $220 million a year. In 2005, Kawakubo told the *New Yorker* magazine that she "never intended to start a revolution," only to show "what I thought was strong and beautiful. It just so happened that my notion was different than everybody else's."

Eunice Kennedy Shriver

∞ Leading Light of the Special Olympics ∞

"Looks fade.
Brains don't."
—*Eunice Kennedy Shriver*

Eunice Kennedy and her sister Rosemary grew up playing sports together: swimming, sailing, skiing, and playing football. Eunice went on to become a college athlete. But Rosemary had been born with a developmental disability. At the time, there weren't programs to help people with disabilities and provide them with opportunities to succeed. Eunice would make changing that her life's mission.

FAMILY TIES

When Eunice was growing up in the 1930s, people with cognitive disabilities were scorned and ignored. Most were sent off to spend their lives in institutions. When the Kennedy family saw that Rosemary was slow to crawl, walk, and speak, they knew she had an intellectual disability, but they refused to send her away. It took a lot of patience and extra work, but they included her in sing-alongs around the piano and made her part of their crew in boat races. But as Rosemary got older, it became more difficult to take care of her. She grew irritable, and her memory seemed to be getting worse. At the urging of Rosemary's doctors, the Kennedys finally found a home for Rosemary that specialized in the care of people with disabilities. But the experience made Eunice wonder if things could have been different for her sister.

Eunice married Robert Sargent Shriver and in 1957 became the executive vice president of an organization established in his honor. She knew exactly what she wanted to do with her new position: use it to help people like Rosemary.

- **BORN:** July 10, 1921, Brookline, Massachusetts, U.S.A.
- **DIED:** August 11, 2009, Hyannis, Massachusetts, U.S.A.
- **LED:** Championing equal rights for disabled people
- **REMEMBERED FOR:** Founding the Special Olympics

A DETERMINATION TO HELP

In 1962, Shriver's telephone rang. It was a woman who had heard about Shriver's advocacy for people with intellectual disabilities. The woman was frustrated that she couldn't find a summer camp that would admit her child, and she wanted Shriver to know. Shriver didn't hesitate to jump in and help, telling the woman to give her a month to find a solution. One month later, Camp Shriver opened at Shriver's home in Maryland. She developed activities for the children inspired by games she had played with Rosemary growing up, and she even jumped in the pool herself to give swimming lessons.

Then, tragedy struck the Kennedy family. Shriver's brother President John F. Kennedy was assassinated in November 1963. Five years later, her brother Robert "Bobby" Kennedy, who was poised to follow in John's footsteps and run for president, was assassinated, too. The double tragedy rocked the nation and sent the Kennedy family reeling. But grief didn't stop Shriver from pushing toward her goal.

SPORTS FOR ALL

In 1968, she founded a new program: the Special Olympics. Shriver believed that if people with disabilities were given the same opportunities as everyone else, they could accomplish more than was thought possible. The Special Olympics was her way to prove that. The first Special Olympics brought together 1,000 athletes from the United States and Canada, and it was an enormous success. Today, nearly six million athletes from more than 170 countries compete in sports from basketball to snowboarding, and Special Olympics events are held around the world every day.

In 1984, Eunice Kennedy Shriver received the Presidential Medal of Freedom—the highest civilian award in the U.S.— and in 2008, *Sports Illustrated* presented her with its first Sportsman of the Year Legacy Award. In May 2009, she became the first non-president or first lady to have her portrait hung at the National Portrait Gallery, in Washington, D.C. Through her lifetime of work, Shriver helped change negative attitudes about people with disabilities.

Eunice Kennedy Shriver speaks with the director of a school for children with disabilities in Bonn, Germany, in June 1963.

COMMANDING KINGS

King of the Peace Corps

John F. Kennedy (1917–1963)

The youngest president ever elected, JFK served at a crucial time during the Cold War—a period of intense superpower rivalry between the United States and the former Soviet Union—and the height of the civil rights movement, which he helped by championing laws against discrimination. Before he negotiated with the Soviet Union to pull the world back from the brink of nuclear disaster and revved up the U.S.-Soviet race to explore space, JFK (along with Eunice Kennedy Shriver's husband, Robert Sargent Shriver) founded the Peace Corps: As one of his first acts in office, he recruited an "army" of civilian volunteers to travel to nations in need. Since then, volunteers— who generally serve for two years—have worked side by side with the people of these nations to build schools and sewer systems, teach classes, and protect the environment. More than 230,000 Americans have served to date.

SOVEREIGNS OF SPORTS

⧫ *Winning Women* ⧫

Every now and then, an athlete comes along that changes the history of her sport forever. The women on this page are more than Olympians and record holders. They're the indisputable queens of their sport—and we, their screaming fans and loyal subjects, bow before their greatness.

Queen of the Court: Serena Williams (1981–)

One of the greatest athletes of all time, Serena Williams has won 23 Grand Slam singles titles, more than any other tennis player in modern history. In comparison, the winningest male tennis player, Roger Federer, has snagged 18. What makes Williams queen of the court? Her feet are fast, and her forehand and backhand are both powerful and accurate. Her serve tops out at 128.6 miles an hour (207 km/h), and she's three times more likely to deliver an ace (a serve her opponent can't return) than any other female tennis pro. Williams started playing tennis at age three, taught by her father, who learned about the sport from books and videos. Before she had graduated from high school, she was one of the top 100 female players in the world. She's changed the face of tennis forever—and she's not done dominating the court yet.

Queen of the Beam: Simone Biles (1997–)

At four feet nine inches (1.4 m), she may be small even for a gymnast, but her performance makes her tower over the competition. Simone Biles sprints powerfully across the mats, giving her more time in the air to flip and spin on the floor and vault. And with her confident demeanor, she makes flying through the air look easy. She was already the three-time defending gymnastics world champion before the 2016 Summer Olympics in Rio de Janeiro, Brazil, where she led the U.S. Women's team to the gold and dominated the competition, scooping up first-place medals in vault, floor, and individual all-around events. With 19 Olympic and World Championship medals, she is the most decorated American gymnast in history.

Queen of the Climb:
Ashima Shiraishi (2001–)

Ashima Shiraishi has been called the most talented rock climber of all time. That's pretty impressive for someone who earned that title before she was even 15 years old! Shiraishi discovered rock climbing at age six, when the New York City native saw people scrambling up a boulder called Rat Rock, in Central Park. She won her first competition at age 7, competing against adult female climbers. At 14, she completed a V15 boulder, considered the most difficult rock climbing challenge, on Japan's Mount Hiei. She was the first woman and the youngest person in history to achieve the feat. Her small, strong fingers and toes and light frame allow her to cling to holds in the rock almost too small to see. But her real talent comes from her ability to concentrate as she swings her body up sheer rock faces. And she's just getting started.

Queen of the Heptathlon:
Jackie Joyner-Kersee (1962–)

Competition for the title of best female athlete of all time is stiff. But many think that honor should go to Jackie Joyner-Kersee. Her event was heptathlon, which combines seven sports in one: a 100-meter (328-ft) hurdle race, the high jump, the shot put, a 200-meter (656-ft) race, the long jump, the javelin throw, and, to finish it off, an 800-meter (2,625-ft) race. Testing speed, flexibility, precision, and brute strength, heptathlon might just be the toughest event in the Olympic Games. And Joyner-Kersee excelled at it. After coming in second in the 1984 Olympic Games due to a torn hamstring, Joyner-Kersee went on to win three golds, a silver, and two bronzes total in the heptathlon and long jump in four successive Olympic Games from 1984 to 1996—the most medals of any woman in Olympic track and field history. She still holds the world record for the heptathlon—and the next five highest scores, too.

COMMANDING KINGS

King of the Dive
Greg Louganis (1960–)

American athlete Greg Louganis is generally considered the greatest diver in history. With his signature elegant twists and flips, he won 13 world championships and five Olympic medals—including one for a perfect score, the first in Olympic diving history. But Louganis's life started out far from perfect: He had a rocky relationship with his adoptive parents and was bullied in school for his dark skin and his struggles with dyslexia, a learning disorder. Luckily, Louganis found something he was good at: diving. He started competing at age nine and won a silver medal at his first Olympics when he was just 16. The 1988 Games were his most challenging of all: Just before the competition, he was diagnosed with HIV. Then, during the preliminaries, he hit his head on the diving board so badly he needed stitches. But Louganis couldn't be stopped. He came back to win two gold medals. Today, he's a motivational speaker, LGBTQ activist, and athlete mentor. He's even made a splash with his new hobby—competing with his beloved dogs in agility trials.

Margaret Bourke-White

∾ Courageous Camerawoman ∾

From the time Margaret Bourke-White was a child, she knew she wanted to do something different with her life. "I pictured myself as the scientist, going to the jungle, bringing back specimens for natural history museums," she said later. Although she didn't become a scientist, she did blaze a new trail for women—as one of America's most renowned photojournalists.

During college in the 1920s, Bourke-White made money on the side selling pictures of the Cornell University campus. When her photographs earned praise, Bourke-White cobbled together a studio in a Cleveland, Ohio, apartment in 1928 and made it her mission to get inside the city's steel mills—which were closed to women—to photograph the factories at work. Those photographs earned her a position at *Fortune* magazine: She became their first photographer ever, male or female. In 1963, she became the first woman to hold a staff photographer position at *Life*, a hugely popular magazine known for its photography.

Bourke-White became known for her incredible bravery on the job. When World War II began, she boarded a transport ship to photograph the fight against fascism. Her ship was torpedoed and sank, and Bourke-White barely made it to a lifeboat clinging to one of her cameras. She covered almost the entire war, crawling on the ground beside soldiers on the Italian front while enemy fire rained down around her. In 1951, she was in a helicopter snapping photos of U.S. Navy practice rescues when it crashed into the Chesapeake Bay. When the Korean War broke out, Bourke-White spent nine months on the front, surviving typhoons, ambushes, and attacks by guerrilla soldiers to snap photos. Even a diagnosis of Parkinson's disease in 1954 couldn't stop her: Bourke-White continued to tell stories with her photos until her death, in 1971.

> "Work is something you can count on, a trusted, lifelong friend who never deserts you."
> —*Margaret Bourke-White*

Royal Rundown

❀ **BORN:** June 14, 1904, New York, New York, U.S.A. ❀ **DIED:** August 27, 1971, Stamford, Connecticut, U.S.A. ❀ **LED:** Photojournalism abroad
❀ **REMEMBERED FOR:** A staggering collection of photographs covering decades

Dorothea Lange

∾ Lady of the Lens ∾

During the 1920s, photographer Dorothea Lange was running a successful portrait studio in San Francisco. But when the Great Depression took hold after the 1929 stock market crash, she couldn't simply sit by. Lange dragged her large Graflex camera out of her studio and onto the streets to capture the struggles people were enduring: losing their homes, waiting hours in line for bread or work, and relying on soup kitchens for food. It was the beginning of a career she would spend using her lens to bring attention to the downtrodden.

Lange was born in 1895 in Hoboken, New Jersey, U.S.A. At age seven, she came down with polio. Back then, there was no vaccine for the virus, and like many children of the time, Lange was left with partial paralysis—hers in her right leg and foot. But when she grew up, Lange saw the experience as a gift that helped her empathize with her subjects. After photographing people coping with the Great Depression in San Francisco, Lange began to travel throughout the United States to document the hardship people across America were experiencing. In 1936, Lange visited a camp of migrant pea pickers who were out of work because the crop had frozen. Lange snapped a photo of a young woman who had sold the tires from her car to buy food for her seven children. The photo, titled "Migrant Mother," became the most iconic picture of the Great Depression.

In 1941, Lange became the first woman to be awarded the prestigious Guggenheim Fellowship for her photography. But she gave up the award so she could photograph the forced relocation of Japanese Americans after the U.S. entered World War II, when more than 100,000 were evacuated from their homes and sent to internment camps. Lange is remembered today as someone who helped shine a light on the plight of overlooked people, capturing their dignity and humanity in the face of extremely difficult circumstances.

> "Photography takes an instant out of time, altering life and holding it still."
> –Dorothea Lange

Royal Rundown

❉ **BORN:** May 26, 1895, Hoboken, New Jersey, U.S.A. ❉ **DIED:** October 11, 1965, San Francisco, California, U.S.A. ❉ **LED:** Photojournalism at home ❉ **REMEMBERED FOR:** Impressive documentation of humanity in some of America's darkest times

Powerful Portrait

It's one of the most famous images of any monarch in history. Called the Armada Portrait, this painting shows Queen Elizabeth I (p. 12), who ruled England and Ireland from 1558 until her death in 1603. Elizabeth was not only a famous queen; she was also a fashion icon whose subjects closely copied her style—huge neck ruff included! But this painting wasn't meant to just show off the queen's fabulous outfit: It's packed with symbols of her mighty influence.

Moment of Victory

The Armada Portrait was painted by an unknown artist around 1588, and it commemorates one of Elizabeth's finest moments: fending off the Spanish Armada, a fleet of 130 ships that sailed from Spain trying—and failing—to invade England in May 1588. The window on the left side of the painting shows the Armada's arrival, and the right-hand window shows its defeat.

Bows and Pearls

Elizabeth was known for making a statement with her clothing. In the Armada Portrait, she shows off her status by wearing all her royal finery, with intricate stitching, adorned with bows, and decorated with pearls. Pearls, representing purity, were a favorite of the queen's.

Power Pose

Other women painted during this time often posed with hands folded in their laps, wearing a passive expression. But Elizabeth's stance is all about authority: She sits in an open stance with her arms apart, her gaze strong and direct.

Global Conquest

The monarch's right hand rests on a globe, and her hand is placed over the Americas. A queen with ambitions of expanding England's territory, Elizabeth was busy colonizing the Americas at the time her portrait was made. Her fingers extend to other parts of the globe, showing that this remarkable royal wanted to conquer the world.

Elizabeth was 55 years old when this portrait was painted, but you'd never know it! She is shown with a youthful face and bright-red hair, as she appeared in the prime of her life, representing her strength and vitality as queen.

Sea Symbol

On the arm of Elizabeth's chair, there is a carved golden mermaid. In mythology, mermaids sing to lure sailors off-course to their deaths. Some historians think that by including a mermaid in the portrait, the artist was showing Elizabeth's victory over the Spanish sailors.

Chapter Five

MONARCHS OF THE ARTS

Though some of these women did portray queens on stage and screen, most weren't real-life monarchs. Instead, these royals of the arts wielded paintbrushes and microphones. With creativity, not a crown, they inspired generations who would come after them. Some stood front and center, while others crafted their vision from behind the camera. Every one of them broke rules and records to create art that will be remembered long after their reigns are over.

International superstar Beyoncé
performing in Milan, Italy

Helen Mirren

∾ Leading Lady ∾

Helen Mirren is the only actress to ever play both Queen Elizabeth I and Queen Elizabeth II.

She's most famous for her Oscar-winning 2006 performance as Queen Elizabeth II (p. 59)—just one of six times she's played a queen over the years. But Helen Mirren isn't just a make-believe monarch: She's Hollywood royalty whose 50-year career on the stage and screen has made her one of the most revered actresses alive today.

DREAM COME TRUE

Many people think of Helen Mirren as the ultimate British actress. But though she was born in London to a British mother, her father was a Russian taxi driver, and her birth name was Ilyena Lydia Mironoff. Mirren discovered her love for acting early on: At age 13, she went to an amateur production of William Shakespeare's *Hamlet* and was captivated by the drama of the stage. Mirren's parents discouraged her, saying acting was no way to make a living. But a teacher at Mirren's high school encouraged her to audition for a youth theater troupe, and at age 18, she was accepted. By her early 20s, Mirren was starring in stage productions, playing famous roles such as Lady Macbeth (p. 44) and Cleopatra (p. 53). In 1968, Mirren made her film debut with *A Midsummer Night's Dream*, a movie

Royal Rundown

❀ **BORN:** July 26, 1945, London, England ❀ **LEADS:** The stage and screen
❀ **KNOWN FOR:** Her dramatic works, including film, stage, and television

adaptation of Shakespeare's famous comedy. Though the stage has always been Mirren's true love, she earned accolades for her performance on the screen, too. She quickly went on to star in dozens of other movies and TV shows. In 1992, she landed her breakthrough role as the lead in the British police drama *Prime Suspect*. Just two years later, she was nominated for an Oscar for her performance as Queen Charlotte in *The Madness of King George*. As time passed, Mirren's career only built up steam. She is one of only 22 actors in history to win the "Triple Crown" of acting—a Tony, Emmy, and Oscar. In 2003, real-life queen Elizabeth II honored her with the title Dame Commander of the Order of the British Empire—the female equivalent of a knighthood.

Helen Mirren as Queen Charlotte in 1994's *The Madness of King George* (left) and in a stage production in London of Shakespeare's *Antony and Cleopatra* (above) in 1998

BETTER WITH TIME

Being older doesn't keep most male actors from earning starring roles. But the same isn't true for women. It's a rare actress who can find consistent work after her 30s. But Mirren has left that age barrier far behind her: At age 67, she starred as a retired assassin in the action-comedy *Red*. And though she's in her 70s now, she shows no signs of slowing down her career.

Mirren is known for speaking her mind to journalists, and she's not afraid to talk about taboo subjects—like her decision to not have children—or to call Hollywood "outrageous" for its double standard for male and female actresses. In a culture of judgment and criticism, Mirren is always unapologetically herself. "Being me right now is sort of amazing," she has said.

COMMANDING KINGS

Screen King
Peter O'Toole (1932–2013)

Peter O'Toole played many kings on stage and screen during his 50-year career. He was nominated for an Oscar for his portrayal of Henry II—twice!—and lit up the stage as Shakespeare's *Hamlet* in 1963. O'Toole also played the ruthless ruler—and husband of Eleanor of Aquitaine (p. 15)—in both 1964's *Becket* and 1968's *The Lion in Winter*. Born in Ireland in 1932, O'Toole set Hollywood abuzz when he portrayed famed British archaeologist, diplomat, and writer T. E. Lawrence in 1962's *Lawrence of Arabia*. The film took two years of filming in seven different countries, but all that work was worth it: It won the Oscar for best picture. After that, O'Toole had his choice of leading roles. He received eight Oscar nominations over his illustrious career. He never won, making him the most nominated actor without a win in the history of film. In 2002, Hollywood honored his life spent spellbinding spectators with an honorary Oscar.

MORE REEL QUEENS

～ *Rulers of the Silver Screen* ～

They're sovereigns of the cinema, princesses of the pictures, and monarchs of movies. These actresses followed their passion for drama to make some of the biggest careers in Hollywood history. For many, the path was a tough one—but they forged ahead anyway, blazing a trail for future actresses to follow.

Regal Trailblazer:
Rita Moreno (1931–)

Rita Moreno is the first Latina to win all four of the major annual entertainment awards in the United States: an Emmy, a Grammy, an Oscar, and a Tony. Moreno knew she belonged in front of a camera—so much so that she began pursuing her dream as a teenager. Her talent impressed Hollywood executives and audiences alike, but it took years of hard work and many auditions before she landed her career-defining role, as Anita in 1961's *West Side Story*. Even after Moreno won the Oscar for her performance, however, she found that she still wasn't being offered diverse film roles. Nevertheless, she continued to shine on film, TV, and the stage, earning praise for her roles in the 1976 comedy *The Ritz*, the 1980s TV show *9 to 5*, and many others. Her groundbreaking work opened doors for actors of diverse backgrounds, and she was awarded two of America's highest honors: the Presidential Medal of Freedom in 2004 and the National Medal of Arts in 2009.

Ruler and Rule Breaker:
Katharine Hepburn (1907–2003)

Over a career spanning nearly 70 years, Katharine Hepburn earned 12 Academy Award nominations and won four best actress Oscars, more than anyone before her. She's known for her portrayals of strong women, including several queens, like *Eleanor of Aquitaine* (p. 15) in *The Lion in Winter* and Mary I (p. 40) in *Mary of Scotland*. But it wasn't just her acting skills that made her famous; it was her confidence and outspokenness. She was unconventional, refusing to give interviews or wear makeup when she didn't feel like it. And though pants were considered unladylike for women at the time, Hepburn liked slacks and didn't give a hoot about what anyone else thought. When the costume department at her production studio went so far as to steal her pants to keep the actress from wearing them, Hepburn one-upped her overbearing bosses and walked around the studio in her underwear.

Queen of Characters:
Viola Davis (1965–)

Viola Davis is the first African-American performer to have won Tony, Oscar, and Emmy Awards for acting roles. But the road to recognition wasn't easy. Davis grew up poor in Rhode Island, U.S.A., where she lived in rodent-infested homes and searched through garbage cans for food. She took her mind off her family's financial troubles by acting, starting with a community play when she was nine years old. Davis proved her chops early, attending Juilliard, a prestigious performing arts school in New York City, then making a name for herself in the New York theatre world, winning her first of two Tony awards in 2001. But she found herself limited to small film and TV roles until 2009, when Hollywood finally recognized her talent. Since then, Davis has made more than 20 films, winning numerous awards, including an Oscar in 2017 for her role in *Fences.* She has also played leading TV roles, earning an Emmy for one of them.

First Lady of Film:
Meryl Streep (1949–)

She's heart-wrenching in dramas and hilarious in comedies, and she never misses a high note in musicals. Many consider Meryl Streep to be one of the world's greatest living actresses. After graduating from the Yale School of Drama in 1975, Streep got her start in acting on the New York stage, then broke into films in the late 1970s. Streep earned her first Oscar nod in 1978, when she was nominated for best supporting actress for her role in the film *The Deer Hunter* alongside Robert De Niro. She's known for her incredible range, portraying all kinds of characters from a Polish survivor of a Nazi concentration camp to beloved chef Julia Child (p. 160). Now in her 70s, she continues to play starring roles—unusual in Hollywood today—and earns more awards and accolades with every one.

Lady of Laughs:
Lily Tomlin (1939–)

Lily Tomlin is a comedy legend whose wacky characters and knack for a perfect punch line have kept audiences in stitches throughout her long career. As a kid growing up in Detroit, Michigan, U.S.A., Tomlin admired female comics like Lucille Ball, star of the *I Love Lucy* show. She studied medicine at Wayne State University, but she never lost her love for the screen. In 1965, she left college to pursue an acting career. She moved to New York City, started performing at comedy clubs, and never looked back. A few years later, she joined the cast of TV sketch comedy show *Laugh-In,* creating zany characters like a snarky telephone operator named Ernestine. Audiences fell in love with Tomlin, and she continued to wow in television comedy specials, stage productions, late-night shows, and films. In 2013, she married her longtime love of 43 years, Jane Wagner, proving that Hollywood relationships can stand the test of time.

Aretha Franklin

～ Queen of Soul ～

> "R-E-S-P-E-C-T. Find out what it means to me."
> —*Aretha Franklin*

One of the most distinctive people in popular music, Aretha Franklin was the unmistakable voice behind hits like "Respect" and "Chain of Fools." She performed for more than 60 years, and people across generations recognize and adore her groundbreaking sound.

Franklin's childhood was marked by tragedy: Her parents separated when she was six, and her gospel-singer mother died four years later. But Franklin found solace in music. She got her start singing in front of her preacher father's congregation, who knew right away they were in the presence of a voice like no other. By age 14, Franklin was recording tracks, and her first album was released in 1956. Franklin went on tour on the gospel circuit, where she met music legends including Sam Cooke, a former gospel singer who had recently switched over to a new genre: pop. Franklin was mesmerized by the new sound. In 1961, she signed a five-year contract with Columbia Records, and she released a string of jazz-pop albums. But her true talent was finally unleashed in 1967, when "Respect" was released and the world got an earful of the power of Franklin's pipes. Her unique sound had spawned a brand-new musical genre: soul. And Franklin became its queen.

After that, nearly everything Franklin recorded became a hit. Her powerful voice came to the fore during the 1960s and 1970s, a time of change for the United States. When the world mourned civil rights icon Martin Luther King, Jr., Franklin sang in tribute at his funeral. Over the course of her career, she won 18 Grammy Awards, making her one of the most honored artists of all time. In 1985, in recognition of her 25th year in the music industry, the state of Michigan declared her voice a "natural resource"; in 1987, she became the first woman inducted into the Rock and Roll Hall of Fame. Franklin's passionate, fiery voice made her an icon, and her songs have been the soundtrack to more than one movement.

Royal Rundown

❀ BORN: March 25, 1942, Memphis, Tennessee, U.S.A. **❀ DIED:** August 16, 2018, Detroit, Michigan, U.S.A. **❀ LED:** Soul music **❀ REMEMBERED FOR:** Creating a new musical genre with her powerful voice

Dolly Parton

❧ Queen of Country ❧

"Find out who you are and do it on purpose."
—*Dolly Parton*

Dolly Parton grew up on a farm in Appalachia, a mountainous area in eastern North America, with 11 brothers and sisters. The family may not have had much money, but they were rich in musical talent: Six of Parton's siblings would go on to work as professional musicians. Parton learned about music by singing in church and started playing on a homemade guitar at age seven. She began singing professionally when she was just 10 years old, appearing on local TV and radio shows in Knoxville, Tennessee. By the time she was 21, her songs were getting noticed. Parton went on to record more than 20 number one country hits, including "Jolene" and "9 to 5." She parlayed her string of hits into a headline act in Las Vegas and started appearing in films, including *Steel Magnolias*, the 1989 hit about a sassy group of Southern women and the bond they share.

Parton backs her musical talent with serious smarts. She's the writing power behind many of her hit songs, and—unlike many artists—she has carefully held on to the publishing rights to her catalog of work, a savvy business move that has earned her a fortune. These days, Parton uses her fame and success to support LGBTQ rights, natural disaster relief efforts, and literacy. She inspires a love of reading through Dolly Parton's Imagination Library, a book-gifting program that mails more than a million free books every month to kids from birth to age five in the U.S., the U.K., Canada, and Australia.

Royal Rundown

❀ **BORN:** January 19, 1946, Sevier County, Tennessee, U.S.A. ❀ **LEADS:** Country music ❀ **KNOWN FOR:** An iconic sound and her support of early childhood literacy

MORE CROONING QUEENS

∾ *Voices of Their Generation* ∾

Without these sovereigns of song, modern music wouldn't be the same. With their star power and standout voices, they shaped new genres, made platinum records, and became the voices of their generation.

Queen Bey: Beyoncé (1981–)

She's one of the biggest superstars in music today, but she's about more than just breaking records: She's also a role model for anyone who is inspired by her operatic vocals, her legendary performances, and her powerful business sense. Beyoncé was already showing signs of her future stardom at age seven, when she sang and danced at talent shows in her native Houston, Texas, U.S.A. By age nine, she was performing with her cousin and school friends in the group that would become the popular '90s trio Destiny's Child. The band was a Grammy-winning success, but Beyoncé was clearly the standout star, and by 2001, she had struck out on her own. To date, she has sold an estimated 100 million records as a solo artist, won 22 Grammys, and become one of the world's highest-paid musicians.

Queen of Latin Pop: Gloria Estefan (1957–)

The Latin community calls her "Nuestra Gloria"—"Our Gloria." Born in Havana, Cuba, she fled to the United States with her family when Communist dictator Fidel Castro rose to power. In 1975, she met her future husband, Emilio Estefan, the keyboardist in a band at a wedding she was attending. At the time, there was no Latin music scene in the United States, but the duo changed that. The band they formed together, Miami Sound Machine, brought the dynamic Latin sound to the top of the charts. Their song "Conga" was the first single to break into the pop, dance, black, and Latin charts all at once. Over time, Estefan became the face of Latin music in the United States. Nothing could stop her—not even a 1990 tour bus crash that broke her back. She came back better than ever, and has been performing concerts and making albums ever since.

Queen of Jazz:
Ella Fitzgerald (1917–1996)

Through some of America's toughest times—the Great Depression, segregation, poverty, and war—Ella Fitzgerald's clear, lilting voice brought reassurance and hope. Fitzgerald had a troubled childhood, and by 1934, she was living on the streets alone. She debuted at age 17 at the Apollo Theater in New York City in raggedy clothes. But when she opened her mouth, the audience was stunned. Many have called Fitzgerald's voice the greatest of all time, and it showed even then. She went on to sell more than 40 million albums and win 13 Grammys—the first African-American woman to earn the coveted award. She loved to collaborate, and she performed with some of the greatest musicians in American history: Louis Armstrong, Count Basie, and Frank Sinatra. She's remembered as an American treasure and is called the First Lady of Song.

Queen of Folk:
Joan Baez (1941–)

Her voice defined an era, but she's much more than a singer. Joan Baez is an activist who has spent six decades singing for social justice, civil rights, and pacifism. Born to a Scottish mother and a Mexican father, Baez grew up no stranger to discrimination. When she was 17, her family moved from Staten Island, New York, U.S.A., to Cambridge, Massachusetts, and Baez fell in love with Boston's new folk music scene. At 18, she sang at the Newport Folk Festival, and her soaring soprano stunned the crowd. Her career was launched. Her music was a mix of American styles: blues, lullabies, and cowboy tunes of the Old West. She was passionate about freedom and equal rights, and she sang about peace on the steps of the Lincoln Memorial and protested alongside migrant farm workers. She's an icon of folk—and she's still singing.

COMMANDING KINGS

The King
Elvis Presley (1935–1977)

He's called "the King" for a reason: Elvis Presley was rock-and-roll's first real star, and one of the biggest cultural icons in American history. Born to working-class parents in a two-room house in Tupelo, Mississippi, U.S.A., Presley grew up listening to gospel singers in church. When he was 13, his family moved to Memphis, Tennessee, where he started hanging around the city's blues legends, like B.B. King. He combined these influences, along with his country roots, into a unique sound, and he quickly became a teen icon. Many tried to dismiss him as untalented and a bad influence, but nothing could stop the King from doing his thing. He starred in 33 movies and played sold-out shows all around the country; it is estimated that he has sold more than one billion records worldwide. His appeal is so undeniably potent that even now, more than 40 years after his death, he is still performing: There are more than 85,000 active Elvis impersonators in the United States alone.

Maya Lin

～ Monumental Monarch ～

Twenty-one-year-old Maya Lin was a student studying architecture at Yale University, in New Haven, Connecticut, U.S.A., in May 1981 when she was given the news that would change her life: She had won a prestigious competition to design one of the most important war monuments of modern history.

AN IDEA IS BORN

Born in Athens, Ohio, Lin was in her senior year at Yale when a professor encouraged her to submit her ideas to a public design competition for a national memorial honoring Vietnam War veterans in Washington, D.C. Hers was one of more than 1,400 entries—so many that they had to be gathered together in an airplane hangar to be judged by a jury of architects and sculptors. The entries were submitted anonymously, so the winning designer was a surprise to everyone—but no one was more surprised than Lin herself. At the time, she hadn't even earned her bachelor's degree in architecture—and her design, originally created as an assignment for one of her classes, had earned her only a B!

Lin's design stood out because it was different from many other war memorials: a simple V-shaped wall of black granite sunken into the ground, its shiny surface carved with the names of approximately

The names of eight women—seven nurses from the Army and one nurse from the Air Force—are inscribed on the monument.

Royal Rundown

❀ **BORN:** October 5, 1959, Athens, Ohio, U.S.A. ❀ **LEADS:** Public monument design ❀ **KNOWN FOR:** The Vietnam Veterans Memorial

Millions of people visit the Vietnam Veterans Memorial in Washington, D.C., every year. Many leave flowers, notes, and other items to honor friends or family members whose names are engraved on the wall.

58,000 American service members who died or went missing in action in the war.

CONTROVERSY AND CRITICISM

Not everyone agreed with the competition judges' choice. Many people disliked Lin's design, saying that it only honored the dead and not the living veterans and that its black hue and appearance of sinking into the earth seemed to criticize rather than celebrate them. Twenty-seven congressional representatives even wrote a letter to President Ronald Reagan calling the design a "scar" in the earth and "a political statement of shame and dishonor."

Construction began on the structure in spite of the protests. And when the new memorial was unveiled in Washington, D.C., on November 13, 1982, the controversy faded away. People traveled from far and wide to visit the monument, running their hands along the smooth granite surface and remembering those who were lost in the war. They noticed that its polished surface reflects the viewer, making many feel a personal connection to the monument and what it represents. Since it opened, an average of more than 10,000 people per day have visited the site. It has been called the greatest memorial of the modern era.

AN EYE FOR DESIGN

The Vietnam Veterans Memorial remains Lin's most famous design, but she has gone on to create many structures since then—her later work also powerful in its simplicity. The Civil Rights Memorial in Montgomery, Alabama, which opened in 1989, is composed of a black granite wall inscribed with a single quote from Martin Luther King, Jr., and a large disk inscribed with names of 40 people who died fighting for the equality of all people. Another, dedicated to women at Yale University, the Women's Table (1993), features simple granite blocks engraved with the number of women enrolled in the university every year since 1701. Lin has also been commissioned to create art installations. Her "Storm King Wavefield"—at the Storm King Art Center, a 500-acre (202-ha) sculpture park in Mountainville, New York— transformed grassy hills into a mesmerizing landscape that looks like ocean waves.

Behind the Design

The Vietnam Veterans Memorial got its start when a wounded soldier named Jan C. Scruggs came home after the war ended. The combat was over, but Scruggs faced a new battle: post-traumatic stress disorder, a condition of severe psychological shock that can develop in people who have experienced traumatizing situations. To help with the healing process for him and the three million other Americans who were dealing with the aftereffects of the war, Scruggs and many other veterans and supporters worked hard to persuade Congress to allocate a three-acre (1.2-ha) plot of land on the National Mall for a memorial. By 1981, the cause had earned $8.34 million in donations. Since it was built, the memorial has helped Americans remember, honor, and understand what happened during the fighting. Over the years, visitors have left tens of thousands of artifacts like military medals and photographs at the monument, which are collected and put on display as part of traveling exhibits. And on several occasions, volunteers have gathered at the site to read out loud all the names of the fallen in honor of Veterans Day.

Zaha Mohammad Hadid

∽ Queen of the Curve ∽

"Your success will not be determined by your gender or your ethnicity, but only on the scope of your dreams and your hard work to achieve them."
—Zaha Mohammad Hadid

When she died in 2016, Zaha Hadid left behind a true mark on the world: futuristic buildings with dramatic swooping shapes. Hadid was the most successful female architect of all time, earning the nickname Queen of the Curve.

DIFFERENT DESIGNS

Hadid was born in Baghdad, Iraq. She studied mathematics at the American University of Beirut and then moved to London in 1972 to study architecture. Hadid made a name for herself in 1983 when she won a prestigious competition to design a leisure and recreational center in Hong Kong called the Peak. Her design of artificial cliffs that appeared to hang from a rock face stunned the judges. They didn't know who this young architect was, but they knew she was special.

In the 1980s and early '90s, Hadid struggled to make a name for herself.

Royal Rundown

❀ **BORN:** October 31, 1950, Baghdad, Iraq
❀ **DIED:** March 31, 2016, Miami, Florida, U.S.A.
❀ **LED:** Architecture
❀ **REMEMBERED FOR:** Her innovative architectural masterpieces

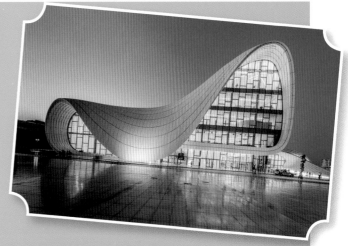

Hadid designed the Galaxy Soho in Beijing, China (above), and the Heydar Aliyev Center (right), in Baku, Azerbaijan.

The Peak was never built, and neither were most of Hadid's other designs. She began to garner a reputation as an architect who made beautiful designs on paper but didn't know much about building in real life. That changed in 1993, when the Vitra Fire Station in Weil am Rhein, Germany, was completed. The building was made up of several angled planes, which together looked like a bird flying. The architecture world took notice, and Hadid began to earn the respect she deserved.

STANDING TALL

Though Hadid was one of very few women architects around, she did not allow her work to be defined by her gender. She fought hard for her unique designs to be judged in their own right. And over time, her work came to be recognized as something truly original. Hadid became famous for curvaceous buildings that seemed to flow across the landscape. Some of her most famous include Michigan State University's Broad Art Museum, and the Guangzhou Opera House in China. Her designs were so groundbreaking that she achieved her goal: Hadid earned a reputation as one of the most celebrated architects of her time.

Hadid went on to win many awards and design all kinds of things, from buildings to glassware, boots, a sofa, and an automobile. In 2004, she became the first woman in history to win the Pritzker Prize, the highest honor in architecture. She became such a celebrity of the field that she was known as a "starchitect." After years of hard work, Hadid finally began to win major commissions in her adopted homeland of Britain. She designed the Aquatics Center for the 2012 Olympics in London. Its wavy roofline is today a city landmark and a bustling neighborhood center for recreational swimmers and kids learning to swim. A walk along the High Line in Manhattan's West Side will bring you up close to Hadid's futuristic condo building at West 28th Street.

When Hadid died at age 65 from a sudden heart attack, the world mourned. Her incredible career was cut short, but in her lifetime, Hadid managed to leave her signature swooping curves on skylines all over the world.

COMMANDING KINGS

Aristocrat of Architecture
Frank Gehry (1929–)

If Zaha Hadid is Queen of the Curve, then Frank Gehry is King. His buildings, composed of arcs and waves in unusual materials, seem to move across the landscape. Today, his structures are some of the most famous and most recognizable ever constructed. But as a young man, Gehry didn't know what he wanted to do with his life. He tried truck driving, radio announcing, and chemical engineering, but his defining moment came in 1977, when he began renovating his own home in Santa Monica, California, U.S.A. (Gehry still lives in the metal-wrapped house today.) Since then, he's gone on to design iconic structures across the world, including the Walt Disney Concert Hall, in Los Angeles, made of a striking series of arcs, and the Guggenheim Museum in Bilbao, Spain, a building made instantly recognizable by its towering titanium swirls.

QUEENS OF THE CANVAS

Many people are skilled with a brush, but few have that special something it takes to show viewers something new. These artists took their experiences—both good and bad—and turned them into art so arresting we still can't stop staring.

Queen of the Southwest:
Georgia O'Keeffe (1887–1986)

She was one of America's most important artists. With her striking images of flowers, landscapes, and bones in the desert, Georgia O'Keeffe founded a new school of art called American modernism. O'Keeffe grew up as one of seven children on a Wisconsin dairy farm. Her teachers noticed her artistic ability early on, and by the time she graduated from high school, O'Keeffe was determined to become a professional artist. In 1915, she began taking natural objects, such as ferns and waves, and simplifying them into abstract shapes and lines. Her work stunned New York gallery owner Arthur Stieglitz, who—unbeknownst to her—put O'Keeffe's drawings on display. The art world took notice, and over the next few years, O'Keeffe became famous. Some of her best known paintings were large-scale images of flowers and scenes from her second home in New Mexico. Today, her works are on display in museums all over the world.

Queen of the Self-Portrait:
Frida Kahlo (1907–1954)

Skilled artist and famous feminist Frida Kahlo turned a life of pain into some of Mexico's most beautiful art. Born in Mexico City, Kahlo contracted polio at age six, which left her with a permanent limp. Then, when she was 18, Kahlo was badly injured when a bus she was riding in crashed. One of the only things she could do while bedridden was paint, and so she did. Even after her recovery, Kahlo confronted her tragedies through her work, painting raw scenes that showed her inner experiences. Kahlo's paintings, many self-portraits, tackled tough topics like gender inequality, infertility, heartbreak, and illness. After she died at age 47, her fame only grew, and when the feminist movement arrived in the 1970s, Kahlo was celebrated as an icon of the independent, creative woman.

Queen of the Impressionists:
Mary Cassatt (1844–1926)

Born into a well-to-do family in Allegheny City, Pennsylvania, U.S.A., in 1844, Mary Cassatt was expected to grow up to be a perfect wife and mother—and nothing more. She was schooled in homemaking, embroidery, sketching, and painting but discouraged from having a career. Undaunted, Cassatt enrolled in art school at age 16 and, in 1866, packed up and headed to Europe (against the wishes of her family) in the hope of learning new skills. For the next 10 years, her ambitions were foiled by the outbreak of war, a shortage of art supplies, and a fire that destroyed many of her paintings. But Cassatt didn't give up: She finally found success in 1879, when she exhibited her work with famous Impressionists like Edgar Degas. In a time when other Impressionists were painting landscapes, Cassatt became known for her portraits of mothers and children in everyday scenes—a groundbreaking subject at the time.

Queen of the Polka Dot:
Yayoi Kusama (1929–)

She's one of the most famous living artists in the world. When she's due to have a new exhibition at a museum, tickets sell out months in advance, and lines can wind around the block. But the path to success was not easy: As a child, Japan-born Yayoi Kusama was plagued by hallucinations. Young Kusama coped by painting what she saw: Her visions of fields of dots became mirrored rooms that made the dotted objects inside seem to stretch to infinity. Throughout her more than six-decade-long career, Kusama has experimented with patterns and repetition, earning her the nickname Queen of the Polka Dot. Through not only her world-renowned mirrored "infinity rooms" but also her painting, fashion, sculpture, performance-based events, and so much more, she has inspired many other pop artists and has been named one of the world's most influential people.

COMMANDING KINGS

King of Cubism
Pablo Picasso (1881–1973)

It seems like Pablo Picasso was born to be an artist: His first word was *piz*, short for the Spanish word for "pencil." Picasso began formal training and drawing and painting at age seven. As a teenager, he would get in trouble at school and be sent to an empty room as punishment, but he loved it; he'd smuggle in a sketch pad and draw for hours. As he reached adulthood—and quickly became famous—Picasso's art never stayed the same for long but tended to switch between radically different styles. One of the most famous was his Blue Period, when the artist, saddened over the death of a friend, painted almost exclusively in blue hues. Another was cubism. In this celebrated style, Picasso depicted people and objects broken apart, disconnected, and floating. This shocking new movement helped set the tone for the art of the 20th century and beyond.

Sister Rosetta Tharpe

～ Ruler of Rock-and-Roll ～

If asked to name the founders of rock-and-roll, most people might list Elvis Presley, Johnny Cash, Little Richard, and Chuck Berry. But they most likely wouldn't include the woman those icons listed as *their* inspiration: Sister Rosetta Tharpe. Most have never heard her name, but rock-and-roll wouldn't exist without her.

Born Rosetta Nubin into a family of religious singers, Tharpe was playing the guitar at just four years old. By the age of six, she was performing on the road with her mother's evangelical troupe. As she grew up, she expanded her style beyond spiritual music and added in Delta blues and New Orleans jazz to craft a totally new sound. Women guitarists were a rare sight in the 1930s, and Tharpe's style was even more unusual: She strummed with energy and confidence, even inventing a technique called the "windmill" often attributed to later male rock stars Keith Richards and Pete Townshend. She sang frankly about love and relationships in a time when those were taboo topics, and audiences sometimes found her scandalous. But Tharpe was determined to keep experimenting, and, by the time she was 23, she had scored her first single.

As a black woman making her way in the 1940s, Tharpe faced unspeakable racism. She toured the United States and Europe to perform for packed venues but had to sleep on buses and pick up food from the back end of restaurants because hotels and restaurants were segregated. All the while, Tharpe kept singing. She was the first gospel musician to sign a recording contract, the first to play at the Apollo Theater in New York City, the first to do a major international tour. With every obstacle against her, Tharpe forged her own path and created a sound that changed music and inspired famous performers who would come after her.

> "All this new stuff they call rock-and-roll, why, I've been playing that for years now."
> —Sister Rosetta Tharpe

Royal Rundown

BORN: March 20, 1915, Cotton Plant, Arkansas, U.S.A. **DIED:** October 9, 1973, Philadelphia, Pennsylvania, U.S.A. **LED:** Rock-and-roll **REMEMBERED FOR:** "Strange Things Happening Every Day," one of the earliest rock-and-roll recordings

Joan Ganz Cooney

❦ Sovereign of Sesame Street ❧

Few know her name, but nearly every kid in America is a big fan of her work. Joan Ganz Cooney observed that few children's programs on TV were fun enough to keep kids interested. But Cooney changed all that when she created the most beloved kid's program in history: *Sesame Street*.

After growing up in Arizona, Cooney earned a degree in education from the University of Arizona in 1951. At the age of 23, she moved to New York City, where she got her first experience in television, producing documentaries. Cooney won an Emmy for her work, but she wanted something more: She wanted to make a difference in people's lives, and she thought perhaps there was a way to use television to educate, not just entertain. Cooney interviewed experts in education, television, and child development and found that disadvantaged children often came to school without a basic knowledge of letters and numbers … and that those same kids watched an average of 27 hours of TV every week. Cooney wanted to harness that viewing time and turn it into learning time. So Cooney spent the next two years raising money and developing her show. Along the way, she became one of America's first female television executives when she was named director of the Children's Television Workshop in 1968. The following year, *Sesame Street* launched.

With its setting on city streets and its diverse cast of characters, *Sesame Street* reflected the lives of many of the kids who were watching. The show was a huge hit and, five decades later, it still is. It's estimated that 77 million Americans have watched the series as children. Guided by Cooney's vision, *Sesame Street* uses humor and songs to teach kids all kinds of skills—from naming colors and letters to dealing with bullies and coping with divorce.

"It's very hard for me to look back; I'm constantly involved in the next thing."
—Joan Ganz Cooney

Royal Rundown

👑 **BORN:** November 30, 1929, Phoenix, Arizona, U.S.A. 👑 **LEADS:** Children's programming 👑 **KNOWN FOR:** Developing the world of *Sesame Street*

Winning Women

It is just 13.5 inches (35 cm) high—not very big as trophies go! But the golden Oscar statuette, standing tall and grasping a sword between its hands, is often called the most recognizable award in the world. Since the first Academy Awards banquet, in 1929, more than 3,000 actors and filmmakers have proudly held their Oscars aloft. Here are some of film history's most famous first-place females.

1957: Miyoshi Umeki

As a kid growing up on the Japanese island of Hokkaido, Miyoshi Umeki dreamed of making it big as a performer across the Pacific Ocean in the United States. She practiced nonstop—even singing with a bucket over her head to keep from annoying her family! She moved to the United States in 1955 and lived out her dream, becoming a singer and actress on TV variety shows. In 1957, she took on the role that made her a superstar: the wife of an American airman in 1957's *Sayonara*. She won an Academy Award for best supporting actress, making her the first—and only—Asian actress to ever win an Oscar.

1940: Hattie McDaniel

In the movies of the 1930s, the only roles open to African-American actors were usually those of servants. When actress Hattie McDaniel was criticized for playing a stereotype, she shot back, "I'd rather play a maid than be a maid." She took on the role at least 74 times, most famously as the sharp-tongued character Mammy in the smash 1939 hit *Gone With the Wind*. When she marched onto the stage to accept her Oscar for best supporting actress, McDaniel made history as the first ever African-American actor to win an Academy Award.

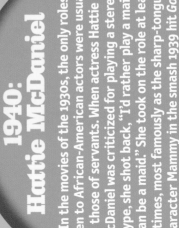

1987: Marlee Matlin

Marlee Matlin lost her hearing when she was a toddler, but she didn't let that stop her from pursuing an acting career. At age 19, she earned a role in a stage production of the play *Children of a Lesser God* and was later cast as the star of the 1986 film version, a movie for adults. For her performance, she won the Oscar for best actress in a leading role—the only person with a disability to attain the award to date.

2010: Kathryn Bigelow

Women have been in charge of movie sets since 1896, when French woman Alice Guy-Blaché became the first female director in the history of film. But it would take more than a century after that before a female film director's work was recognized with an Academy Award: That history-maker was Kathryn Bigelow, who directed *The Hurt Locker*—a film for adults about the Iraq war.

1974: Tatum O'Neal

Born in 1963 in Los Angeles, California, Tatum O'Neal rocketed into stardom at the age of 10 when she won an Academy Award for best supporting actress in the film *Paper Moon*. She shared the screen with her father, actor Ryan O'Neal, and the duo was applauded for their on-screen connection playing a father and daughter during the American Great Depression. The win made O'Neal the youngest person ever to receive an Oscar.

1994: Whoopi Goldberg

In 1991, comedian and actress Whoopi Goldberg accepted the Oscar statuette for best supporting actress for her role in the movie *Ghost*. That made her the first African-American woman to earn the honor in nearly 50 years, since Hattie McDaniel. But Goldberg wasn't done breaking Oscar records yet: She went on to host the show in 1994—and then again in 1996 and 1999—the first woman ever to do so.

© A.M.P.A.S.

Chapter Six

LEGENDARY LEADERS

For thousands of years, storytellers have spun tales of queens who ruled kingdoms from golden thrones. Stories of these powerful rulers have kept generations of audiences on the edge of their seats. Some of them are fictional. But others were real-life ladies who led armies and conquered kingdoms. Read on to learn more about queens so incredible their stories became the stuff of legend.

Actress Gal Gadot played the title character in 2017's *Wonder Woman,* a film based on the DC Comics superhero and member of the Amazons, legendary warrior women.

Esther

∾ Queen of Persia ∾

Some scholars believe she was a real person. Others think she was a character made up to teach lessons in the Bible. But fact or fiction, Esther is an important religious figure and an icon to the Jewish people. Esther started out as an exiled Jew but rose above her circumstances to save her people and eventually become the queen of Persia. Today she is the hero of the Book of Esther and celebrated during the Jewish holiday of Purim.

FROM EXILE TO QUEEN

Esther was born as Hadassah, a Jewish name that means "myrtle." The myrtle tree would come to symbolize the nation of Israel when Jewish people brought the tree with them as they returned to Jerusalem, the homeland from which they had long been exiled. Small groups of Jews were scattered across the Middle East; among them was Esther's family, in Persia. Esther's parents died when she was a young child, and she was raised by her older cousin Mordecai.

The Book of Esther in the Bible begins when the king of the Persian Empire, Xerxes I, decides to throw an extravagant party. Even though Xerxes ruled over the greatest empire of his time, he was not a wise man. The people of his kingdom feasted for 180 days, and on the final day, Xerxes ordered his queen, Vashti, to appear before the people without her veil on. But Vashti was modest, and she refused. Enraged that his wife would dare to disobey him, Xerxes ordered his counselors to make an example of her, and Vashti was banished.

Royal Rundown

❀ **LIVED:** ca 400s B.C., Persian Empire (modern-day western Asia)
❀ **LED:** Persia ❀ **REMEMBERED FOR:** Advocating for her people

BECOMING A HERO

Xerxes was now in need of a wife, so he ordered all eligible ladies of the land to be brought to his court for him to choose from. The king chose Hadassah (soon to be Esther) as his next queen. What the Persian ruler didn't know was that his chosen bride was Jewish. To protect herself, she took on a new name, Esther, to hide her heritage.

Things seemed to be going smoothly—until the king appointed a new prime minister, named Haman. Haman and Esther's cousin Mordecai didn't get along, because Mordecai refused to bow down to Haman for religious reasons. Haman found out that Mordecai was Jewish and decided to punish Mordecai in the worst way he could think of—by ordering every Jew in Persia to be killed. Terrified, Mordecai begged Esther to use her position to help her people.

Though she was just a young girl, trapped in a marriage to an evil king, Esther steeled herself to be brave. She urged all Jews to fast and pray for their safety. Then, risking her own life, Esther went to King Xerxes. She revealed her Jewish ancestry and told the king about Haman's plot to murder her people. It worked: Xerxes was horrified. He ordered Haman to be executed and decreed that the Jewish people would be forever protected throughout his land. To celebrate, the Jews marked the day with the festival of Purim. And to this day, they honor brave Esther and the deliverance of their people on that day every year.

Esther is depicted in stained glass at St. Mary's Church, in Bury St. Edmunds, Suffolk, England (above), and at her meeting with Xerxes in this painting by 17th-century Italian artist Artemisia Gentileschi (left).

COMMANDING KINGS

The Wise One

King Solomon (ca 990 B.C.–ca 931 B.C.)

Revered in Judaism, Christianity, and Islam, King Solomon is one of the most important figures in the Bible. According to the story, God appeared to Solomon in a dream and offered to grant him anything he wanted. Solomon thought hard and asked God for the ability to lead his people wisely. God was so impressed that he granted the king not only great wisdom but also fabulous riches. Solomon led Israel into a 40-year period of peace and expanded commerce, and undertook massive building projects—among them the temple on Mount Moriah in Jerusalem, one of the marvels of the ancient world. Some experts think Solomon was just a fictional character, but others say he really existed, around the 10th century B.C. Archaeologists on the hunt for evidence of the wise king and his mighty kingdom have discovered sites like a 3,000-year-old defensive wall that seems to correspond to one mentioned in the Bible.

LADIES OF LORE

❧ Storied Queens ❧

They may not have been real people, but these queens of legend loom larger than life. These mythical monarchs have inspired centuries of books, plays, and poems. Stories depict each as fair and beautiful, but they were far from perfect—causing everything from comedic chaos to the downfall of a kingdom.

Queen of Camelot: Guinevere

There are many stories of King Arthur, his beautiful Queen Guinevere, and their mythical court of Camelot that have been told and retold for more than a thousand years. As one version goes, Guinevere was the lovely daughter of the king of Scotland. Though Arthur's magical adviser, Merlin, warned the king that marrying Guinevere would bring about the downfall of his kingdom, Arthur did it anyway. As a wedding gift, Guinevere's father gave Arthur the round table that would come to seat his noble knights. But trouble brewed soon after the marriage, when Guinevere met Lancelot, Arthur's bravest knight. Lancelot and Guinevere fell in love, beginning the most famous love triangle in the history of English literature.

Queen of the Fairies: Titania

Miniature, magical fairies have been part of English folklore for as long as people have been spinning tales. And the queen of these mystical beings is Titania, a character made famous in Shakespeare's *A Midsummer Night's Dream*. In the play, Titania might be no more than a tiny fairy, but she's a force to be reckoned with. Beautiful and gracious, she's also stubborn: At the play's beginning, Titania has agreed to raise an orphaned human boy. When her husband, Oberon, wants to make the boy a guard in his royal fairy troop, Titania refuses to give him up. The conflict between Oberon and Titania drives the mix-ups and misunderstandings of the other characters in the play, which has become one of Shakespeare's most popular works.

Goddess Queen
Dido of Carthage

Famous for founding Carthage, a city in modern-day Tunisia, Africa, this queen's rise to the top is nothing short of legendary. Some historians think Dido's story is based on historical fact, but others think she was a totally fictional figure. Ancient writers tell a tale of a runaway princess who escaped her hometown after her brother threatened to kill her so that he could become king. As she traveled, Dido gained a large following, and by the time she reached North Africa, she decided to settle with them and built a new city on a hill, which she named Carthage. There, she ruled as queen and became so beloved that after she died, the people of Carthage worshipped her as a goddess.

Queen of Britain:
Cordelia

Some tales say King Arthur's ancestry traces back to a legendary queen of Britain named Cordelia. No evidence has ever been found that Cordelia really existed, but her story has been passed down for centuries. As the legend goes, the ancient ruler of Britain was a not-so-noble king named Leir. Leir had three daughters, and when they were old enough, he decided to arrange marriages for them. Two of the daughters flattered him with compliments—but not Cordelia. Angered by his daughter's boldness, Leir refused to give her a piece of his kingdom, all but guaranteeing that she would never marry. Cordelia managed to snag a spouse anyway, a king named Aganippus. But Leir lost his kingdom, and his two loyal daughters turned against him. Desperate, Leir threw himself at Cordelia's feet, begging for her help. She graciously agreed, lending him her army to use to recapture Britain. In gratitude, Leir made Cordelia the heir to his throne. When he died, she became queen of Britain.

COMMANDING KINGS

The Once and Future King
King Arthur (ca 400s)

According to legend, he once defended Great Britain and transformed it into a gleaming kingdom. He will return to do it again. Tales of King Arthur, a warrior king who rose to power after plucking the sword Excalibur from a stone, have been told in the British Isles since the Middle Ages. Experts think Arthur was based on a collection of real-life medieval movers and shakers, inspiring a legend that grew more fantastical through the centuries. If Arthur's knights met at a round table or quested for the Holy Grail (a gold cup said to grant immortal life), such artifacts have never been found. But on a grassy hill named Cadbury jutting

hundreds of feet above the English countryside, archaeologists have discovered evidence of a massive timber castle protected by four ditches that occupied the site in the early Middle Ages. Legend has it that the famous warrior king once sat there, in a kingdom called Camelot.

Marie Laveau

∾ Voodoo Queen of New Orleans ∾

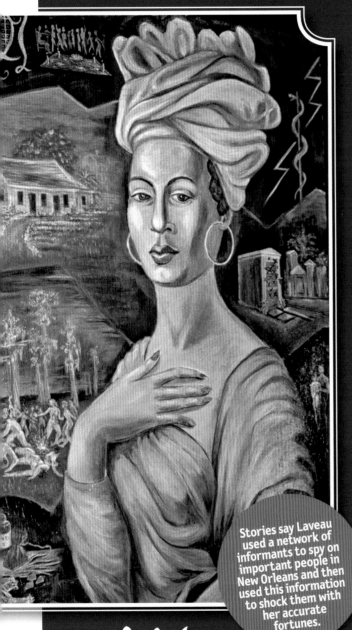

Stories say Laveau used a network of informants to spy on important people in New Orleans and then used this information to shock them with her accurate fortunes.

n the French Quarter district of New Orleans, Louis[iana], U.S.A., tourists flock to one grave in particular in St[.] Louis Cemetery. The tomb is rumored to hold the remains of Marie Laveau, the voodoo queen of New Orleans. Visitors draw X's on the tomb walls (though the p[rac]tice is against local laws) because legends say this queen [can] work her magic beyond the grave to grant their wishes.

Fact mingles with fiction in the story of Marie Laveau[, but] historians believe she was a real person born in the Fren[ch] Quarter around 1801. Like many people of the area, Lavea[u] was said to be a Creole, one of a group of free people of [ ] mixed African and European descent. Many Creole peopl[e] the time practiced voodoo, a religion that combines Afri[can] religious beliefs and Catholic traditions. And Laveau beca[me] its queen. When her husband disappeared, Laveau starte[d] working as a hairdresser to earn money for her family. S[he] listened to her clients' stories about relationships and p[er]sonal affairs and offered advice. Her clients began to bel[ieve] that Laveau could give them more than just guidance: It [was] rumored that she could predict the future, incant a love [ ] spell, and even save prisoners from execution. Laveau so[ld] charms and gris-gris—pouches of mystical herbs, oils, h[air,] nails, and grave dirt.

Over time, Laveau grew to dominate the voodoo wo[rld.] She presided over rituals and, most famously, began ho[ld]ing an annual feast on the banks of Lake Pontchartrai[n in] the 1830s. The ceremony, which took place on the summ[er] solstice, was one of the first times voodoo was practic[ed] not in secret but proudly in public for all to see, Cre[ole] and non-Creole alike. Today, the city still celebrates the event every year on June 23, St. John's Eve, wh[en] guests wearing all white come to the lake's shores bearing gifts in honor of Laveau.

Sammu-ramat

∽ Queen of Babylon ∽

She was the only woman ever to have ruled the Assyrian Empire, the most powerful kingdom in the ancient world from 900 to 600 B.C. She's been immortalized as a legendary figure in paintings, books, and operas—but Sammu-ramat (also known as Semiramis) was a real person whose reign fascinated the world.

Archaeologists have unearthed artifacts they believe to be evidence that the woman behind the myth actually lived in the Assyrian Empire about 2,800 years ago. They've discovered four statues and stone slabs in ancient cities across the Middle East inscribed with the ancient queen's name and tales of her wisdom and her exploits—among them that her husband, King Shamshi-Adad, weakened his empire defending his throne from his older brother. When he died, his son, Adad-nirari, was too young to rule. So the job fell to Queen Sammu-ramat.

She didn't waste any time, immediately embarking on a mission to fill her kingdom with magnificent buildings. Though historians think it's unlikely, legends give her credit for constructing the city of Babylon and its hanging gardens—one of the seven wonders of the ancient world. Next, Sammu-ramat set off to defend her empire, as her armies put an end to uprisings in Persia and North Africa. Then Sammu-ramat set the ambitious goal of invading and capturing India. The campaign was a failure, but one story says that, along the way, Sammu-ramat stopped in Egypt and consulted a prophet, who told her that her son was plotting against her to seize her throne. Putting the peace of her kingdom first, she handed over the kingdom to her son.

Though many historians don't think it's true, legends say Queen Sammu-ramat built the ancient city of Babylon.

Royal Rundown

❀ **LIVED:** ca 9th century B.C. ❀ **LED:** Assyria ❀ **REMEMBERED FOR:** Being a queen who ruled successfully during a time of kings

The Amazons

～ Real-Life Wonder Women ～

In Greek legend, the Amazons were a race of fierce female warriors who lived together in a distant land. For a long time, they were believed to have been no more than a myth. But in recent years, archaeologists have uncovered evidence that the Amazons were real. And the true story is even more amazing than the legend.

THE MYTH

According to Greek mythology, the Amazons were wild warriors who terrified their enemies. They would ride on horseback from their land at the distant edge of the known universe to do battle, holding bows, spears, and axes at the ready. They were led by Hippolyte, the queen of the Amazons, who wore a magical belt given to her by her father, Ares, the god of war.

The Greek historian Herodotus, who lived around the fifth century B.C., penned a tale of a group of female fighters who brawled with the Greeks at a battle along the Thermodon River, in modern-day Turkey. The victors took the women prisoner and put them on their ships. But the Amazons managed to outsmart their captors, escaping and killing them. Since the Amazons were horsewomen unfamiliar with sailing, however, they drifted at the mercy of the winds until they landed on the shores of Crimea,

A marble statue of an Amazon warrior (left) stands in a square in Izmir, Turkey; the ancient Greeks were fascinated with legends of the Amazons and depicted them in art as early as 550 B.C.

Excavation of a football-field-size Scythian burial mound in the republic of Tuva, in Russia

According to comic books, the superhero Wonder Woman was the youngest and most powerful Amazon warrior.

a point of land on the northern edge of the Black Sea. When the nearby settlement of a people called Scythians sent scouts to check out the newcomers, the men were intrigued by the castaways. They fell instantly in love, gave up their settled ways, and joined the Amazons for a nomadic life.

THE TRUTH

Though many stories about the Amazons were surely made up, historians now know that they were real women. The Scythians were a nomadic people who traveled across the Eurasian steppes from about the ninth century B.C. to the first century B.C. When archaeologists excavated Scythian burial mounds, beginning in the early 2000s, they found the remains of a horse-riding people who were clearly warriors buried with their weapons. At first, the scientists assumed these ancient soldiers must be male. But DNA testing revealed something shocking: About one-third of all the remains found belonged to women.

Alongside this incredible find, archaeologists also found a whole armory of weapons: arrows, swords, daggers, spears, armor, and shields. Many of the bodies had sustained war injuries. Historians believed these horse-riding, ferocious fighters had to be the Amazons of so many legends.

According to ancient artwork and literature, the Amazons were a force to be reckoned with: In 1,300 images of Amazons fighting, only two or three show them begging for mercy. They tattooed each other with mythical animals and geometric designs. They wore trousers in loud patterns. And now we know that they were much more than legend: They were real-life women who rode their horses and brandished their bows on the plains of Eurasia long ago.

117

Amina

∾ Conquering Queen ∾

The name Amina means "truthful" or "honest."

The people of Nigeria still tell tales about this legendary warrior queen. But historians think they're more than just stories: They believe Queen Amina was a real person and the first woman to rule Zazzau, part of modern-day Nigeria, more than 400 years ago. To piece together Amina's story, experts have drawn from historical documents and oral legends that have been passed down from generation to generation. They disagree about the details—some are likely true, while others may be exaggerated for the sake of a good story.

BORN TO RULE

One tale says that, as an infant, Amina could wield a dagger as well as any soldier could. That's unlikely, but according to what historians know about her, the tale could hold a bit of truth: Amina was the granddaughter of a king and the daughter of a family that had grown wealthy from the trade of salt, cloth, horses, leather goods, and metals. She grew up with a strong interest in ruling and was educated in government and warfare. When her brother Karama became king in 1566, Amina trained as part of the Zazzau cavalry.

Historians believe that over years of hard training, Amina earned a reputation as a fierce warrior skilled in battle and eventually led the cavalry on military conquests.

Though no woman had ever ruled Zazzau before, Amina was the natural choice to take over from Karama when he died 10 years into his rule. With the respect of the military behind her, Amina became the ruler of Zazzau.

As queen, Amina continued to wage war and conquer new lands. Just a few months after she took the throne, she led an army of 20,000 men into battle to win new territory. With Amina at the front, the army took over towns and won command of trade routes throughout northwestern Africa. Over the years of her reign, Amina expanded her kingdom to the largest size in its history. Experts know this because with each new territory she conquered, Amina ordered her troops to build mighty earthen walls around her new towns and cities to keep the people within safe and protected. Many of those walls stand to this day, in what is now northwestern Nigeria.

FIERCE AND FAMOUS

Amina's military prowess made her kingdom wealthy and powerful. Conquered territories paid her tribute with gold, slaves, and crops. Stories say Amina's troops went into battle wearing iron helmets and chain mail, a sign of wealth. Amina was celebrated throughout the land as a great leader, and today, traditional praise songs still celebrate her conquests, calling her "a woman as capable as a man."

According to historical accounts, there's no evidence that Amina ever married. Some legends say that she went to extremes to keep from sharing the throne; a few tales tell of how Amina took a husband from every new land she conquered. It's uncertain how her reign of 36 years ended, but today, Amina is celebrated as one of the greatest of all northern Nigerian leaders in history. A statue of her stands in Lagos, Nigeria—the largest city on the African continent—depicting the great warrior queen with a sword in her hand, forever ready to do battle.

Amina appears on this commemorative Nigerian postage stamp issued in 1975.

Royal Rundown

* **BORN:** ca 1533, Zaria, Nigeria
* **DIED:** ca 1600, near Bida, Nigeria
* **LED:** Zazzau (now part of Nigeria)
* **REMEMBERED FOR:** Leading her soldiers into battle

COMMANDING KINGS

King of Zulu

Shaka (1787–1828)

Shaka was born a prince, the son of Senzangakhona, king of the Zulu, and his wife Nandi. But when his parents' marriage fell apart, and Shaka and his mother were cast out of Zululand, Shaka didn't just lose his position—the exiled powerless prince became the target of merciless bullying. Determined to get revenge, Shaka became a soldier, then a commander. When his father, the king, died, Shaka saw his chance to take back what was once his. He borrowed an army and marched on Zululand, where he killed the sitting ruler and took the Zulu throne. Shaka quickly impressed his new subjects with his military prowess, outfitting his soldiers with new weapons that made them hard to beat on the battlefield. Less than a year later, the Zulu empire had quadrupled in size.

MYTHICAL MONARCHS

Legendary Women From Around the World

From a goddess shaped like a snake to another whose subjects tamed magical monsters called griffins, these leading legendary deities were feared and loved across the globe.

Empress of California:
Calafia

Long before the state of California was founded, there was a myth about another California: a mythical island ruled by a mighty warrior queen named Calafia. On the island lived beautiful and fierce black female fighters who wielded golden weapons and tamed wild griffins—mythical creatures with the body of a lion and the head and wings of an eagle. No men lived among them, and their ruler was the great Calafia. The myth of Calafia was created in the 1500s, when Spanish author Garci Rodríguez de Montalvo wrote about her in a tale called *The Adventures of Esplandián*. The tale was so popular that explorers like Hernán Cortés took it along on their first voyages to America. Today, the mythical queen is honored as the spirit of the state of California and has been depicted in artworks, stories, and films.

Goddess of Love:
Freya

She's the most famous of all the Norse gods and goddesses, associated with love, beauty, gold, war, and death. Freya's most important role was ruling the afterlife realm Folkvang. According to an old Norse poem, it was her job to choose which warriors killed in battle would spend eternity there. Freya traveled in style: She either rode in her chariot drawn by two cats or put on her cloak of falcon feathers and flew. Freya was known as an expert practitioner of *seidr*, a form of magic, and Norse myths credit her with the evil act of introducing witchcraft to both the gods and the humans. Her biggest weakness was her love for material objects, especially jewelry. So it was fortunate for Freya that when she cried her tears turned to amber or gold.

Snake Goddess: Nu Gua

Ancient art depicts her with a human head but with the body of a snake. In mythology, she was the first queen of China. Nu Gua became the patron saint of matchmakers and was responsible for all rules of conduct between husbands and wives—but she didn't stop there. When an enormous bull called the King of Oxen terrorized the people, it was Nu Gua who controlled him with a magical rope and stopped the destruction. When the pillar supporting the heavens was damaged, it was Nu Gua who repaired it. Her heavenly palace later became the model for China's great walled cities. The earliest Chinese legends say that Nu Gua was the first human being, an independent and powerful goddess who created all of humankind. It was only later that the legends added a male companion, Fu Xi, who ruled by her side.

Queen of Heaven: Ishtar

Ishtar was the most important female deity in ancient Mesopotamia (modern Iraq). Poems with her as the subject were composed more than 4,000 years ago, making her the oldest deity that's ever been written about. Ishtar was the goddess of love, worshipped by everyone from those who wanted to catch the eye of someone special to those who wanted to bring a family closer together. She was also the goddess of war, and on the battlefield, she was so terrifying that she made even the gods tremble in fear. The earliest records of Ishtar were written by Enheduanna—the world's first author known by name, a priestess of the moon god who lived around 2300 B.C. According to Enheduanna's poems, Ishtar was a goddess of opposites: birth and death, beauty and terror, love and war. People in the ancient world worshipped this complex and powerful figure for thousands of years.

COMMANDING KINGS

Chief Deity
Zeus

As king of all the gods of ancient Greece, Zeus sat atop Mount Olympus dispensing justice and controlling the weather. He was the god of sky and thunder, hurling lightning bolts down on Earth to keep the mortals in line. But Zeus wasn't always on top.

According to Greek lore, Zeus and his brothers and sisters were born from the Titans, beings who existed even before the gods. Fearing the new generation, Zeus's titanic father, Cronus, swallowed all his children. But Zeus survived—hidden from Cronus by his mother, Rhea. When he was fully grown into his powers, Zeus forced Cronus to release the other gods, then led them in a battle against the Titans that lasted for 10 years. Finally, the gods prevailed, and the Titans were locked away in the deepest pit of the underworld. This left Zeus with enough free time to become a father to Greece's greatest hero: Hercules.

Wu Zetian

～ Ambitious Empress ～

According to traditional Confucian beliefs, a female ruler would be as strange as having a "hen crow like a rooster at daybreak." But Wu Zetian—the only woman leader in more than 3,000 years of Chinese history—paid that no mind.

Fact mixes with fiction in her story, but all sources agree that Wu Zetian rose to power by seizing opportunity wherever she saw it—often at the cost of those around her. Starting when she was a young teenager, she served the emperor in the imperial palace. When he died, custom decreed that she should then shave her head and spend the rest of her days in a convent. But instead, Wu Zetian got close to the new emperor. Somehow, she persuaded him to get rid of his wife, the current empress. By A.D. 666, she was ruling as the emperor's equal.

When the emperor died in 683, tradition dictated Wu Zetian couldn't rule on her own as a woman, but she wasn't about to give up her position of power to some other ruler. Wu Zetian and the emperor had had two sons together, so she stood back as one, then the other ascended the throne—all the while controlling them from behind the scenes like a master puppeteer. In 690 she finally forced her second son to step down and let her take the throne instead. When people protested their new female ruler, Wu Zetian simply had them put to death. She used a network of spies to flush out her opponents, and within three years, she had destroyed everyone who had any claim to the throne. Despite her ruthlessness toward those in China's government, her reign was a time of peace and prosperity for the rest of China's 50 million citizens. Wu Zetian's ambition and actions were certainly severe and inhumane, but no more so than those of many male emperors of the time.

Wu Zetian proclaimed herself an incarnation of the Buddha, giving her divine power over her people.

Royal Rundown

BORN: ca 624, Tang Empire, China   **DIED:** December 16, 705, Luoyang, China   **LED:** China   **REMEMBERED FOR:** Plotting her way to power

Tamar of Georgia

～ The Queen Who Was a King ～

The greatest monarch in the history of the Eurasian country of Georgia conquered huge territories, stopped opposing armies in their tracks, and presided over a golden age that has never been equaled. She was also a woman—the first to rule her country. Her power was reflected by her title: king.

Tamar was born in troubled times. Her father, King George III, was surrounded by scheming nobles who plotted to take over the throne. George needed to cement his power. So even though his only child was a girl, he decided to make her king. To help the people accept their first ever female ruler, George and Tamar led the kingdom side by side as co-rulers for six years. Historical accounts differ on how his plan played out. Some say the nobles accepted Tamar as their new ruler with open arms. Other say they rebelled against her leadership—and that Tamar struck the movement down with violent ferocity.

To strengthen her position with the people, Tamar decided to get married. Unfortunately, her husband, a Russian prince named Yuri, turned out to be unworthy. He started wars for no reason and liked to publicly insult Tamar for not bearing him a child. So Tamar stood up for herself. In a time when such a thing was unheard of, with the church strictly opposed, she divorced him. Infuriated, Yuri teamed up with some unhappy nobles and staged a rebellion—which Tamar promptly crushed. Then she expanded Georgia's borders and, in the meantime, supported culture and the arts. When she wasn't on the throne, she found time to fall in love, remarry, and have two children. Today, she's a hero of the Georgian people, who celebrate her every year with a feast on May 24.

To this day, Tamar is one of the most popular names in Georgia.

Royal Rundown

❀ **BORN:** ca 1160, Georgia   ❀ **DIED:** ca 1213, Georgia   ❀ **LED:** Georgia
❀ **REMEMBERED FOR:** Leading her country from pandemonium to prosperity

Storied Sword

A Fable Forged

According to the tale of Sir Thomas Malory, who wrote *Le Morte d'Arthur (The Death of Arthur)* in 1485, King Arthur started out with a different sword, which broke in battle. So the king asked his adviser, the magician Merlin, what to do. Merlin took Arthur to a lake to meet a supernatural being called the Lady of the Lake. While the king and the magician looked on, her hand emerged out of the water in the center of the lake, holding a beautiful sword: Excalibur. The king accepted the blade, and Excalibur would stay by his side for the rest of his reign.

Celtic Lore

Historians think that the figure of the Lady of the Lake may have been based on ancient Celtic stories about water deities. These beings were extremely popular with the Celts, who thought that the movement of water through springs, rivers, and lakes must have been controlled by supernatural fairies who lived under the waves. Ancient people would often leave offerings—including weapons—at important water sites. Modern people continue the tradition today when we toss coins into wishing wells.

Mightier Than Merlin

Merlin is known as perhaps the greatest magician of all time. But in some tales, the Lady of the Lake was far more powerful. When Merlin met the Lady of the Lake, he was so enchanted with her that he agreed to teach her all the secrets of his magic. Eventually, the student surpassed the teacher, and the Lady of the Lake used her sorcery skills to imprison Merlin in a glass tower. Then she took over Merlin's role as King Arthur's chief magical adviser.

Excalibur is probably the most famous sword ever wielded. Lofted by the legendary King Arthur (p. 113), the weapon has figured in many tales of the great king and his noble knights. But did you know that Arthur would never have carried his famous blade if it hadn't been for a legendary woman? She's known as the Lady of the Lake.

Return of the King

Arthur kept Excalibur at his side for many years, winning battle after battle with the weapon until he suffered a mortal wound during the Battle of Camlann. Knowing death was near, Arthur asked one of his knights, Sir Bedivere, to throw the sword into a nearby lake. As the sword flew through the air, a woman's arm arose from the water and grabbed Excalibur out of the air. Arm and sword then slid beneath the surface. According to legend, the Lady of the Lake still guards the blade, deep in one of Britain's lakes.

Social robotics pioneer Dr. Cynthia Breazeal with Maddox, a personal robot she developed

QUEENS
OF KNOWLEDGE

Since ancient times, women have been discouraged—or banned outright—from the world's institutions of learning. But that didn't stop these brave and brainy women. Some lived in the past, when the title of the world's leading mathematician and astronomer belonged to a woman. Others rule the modern day, including female scientists who are making huge strides in solving math problems, saving Earth's wildlife, and discovering new planets.

Hypatia

∽ Queen of Reason ∽

One day around A.D. 415, an angry mob stormed down the streets of Alexandria, Egypt. They were coming for Hypatia. At the time, she was the world's leading mathematician and astronomer—the first woman in recorded history to work in these fields. So who was this leader in logic, and why did she meet such a violent end?

TURBULENT TIMES

Alexandria was the ancient world's center of learning. Founded by Greek ruler Alexander the Great in 331 B.C., it contained a library bursting with half a million scrolls. There, the most brilliant thinkers of the time met to study and to discuss philosophy and the movements of the stars. But by the time Hypatia was born, Alexandria was in decline. The famous library was destroyed—some say Julius Caesar invaded the city in 48 B.C. and accidentally burned it down. Over the next few centuries, religious fighting between Christians, Jews, and pagans plagued Alexandria. But a few scholars pressed on despite the unrest. One was Theon, Hypatia's father. Theon was one of the most educated men in Alexandria, and he was determined that his daughter follow in his footsteps. He taught her to be passionate about searching for answers. He instructed her on the religions of the world. And he coached her to use the power of words to influence people.

Some scholars think that Hypatia's death marked the beginning of the Dark Ages.

Royal Rundown

❀ **BORN:** ca 370. Alexandria, Egypt ❀ **DIED:** ca 415, Alexandria, Egypt ❀ **LED:** Alexandria,
Egypt's academic scene ❀ **REMEMBERED FOR:** Becoming the first female mathematician in history

As depicted in these paintings, Hypatia was a scholar who also shared her ideas with others through public lectures.

THINKER, TEACHER, SPEAKER

Soon, Hypatia's knowledge had surpassed her father's. She discovered a love for mathematics, astronomy, and astrology. She became a skilled speaker and would put on a scholar's robes and deliver public lectures. Soon, people from nearby cities were traveling to hear her thoughts on math and science. She took on students and taught them advanced skills, such as how to build an astrolabe, an instrument used to make astronomical measurements until the 19th century.

Hypatia was also a philosopher. She chose never to marry, instead devoting her life to writing, thinking, and speaking. Her school of philosophy was centered around the idea that there is an ultimate reality beyond the ability of the human mind to understand, something called Neoplatonism. Unfortunately, to the early Christians who were gaining power in Alexandria, Hypatia's belief system was a threat. This conflict would ultimately lead to Hypatia's downfall.

TRAGIC END

Hypatia was highly respected in Alexandria. But her city had more on its mind than math and science: It was embroiled in bloody religious conflict between the old, pagan religion and the new Christianity. A Christian religious leader named Cyril closed down places of worship of other faiths and set about destroying what was left of Alexandria's great library. He led a crowd that chased Jewish people out of Alexandria and looted their homes and temples. Then Cyril turned his attention to his next target: Hypatia, the face of the pagan religion he was trying to crush. An angry mob of Cyril's followers attacked Hypatia and ended her life.

But Hypatia didn't fade from history. The last academic of an enlightened time, she stood for science and reason. And though she lost her life for these beliefs, today she is a symbol of resistance, a feminist icon, and a true inspiration.

COMMANDING KINGS

King of Questions

Socrates (ca 470–399 B.C.)

The ancient Greeks thought the Oracle of Delphi could speak the wisdom of the gods to ordinary people. But when the Oracle said that Socrates was the wisest man in the land, Socrates himself was a little skeptical. A soldier turned philosopher, Socrates set out to investigate the words of the Oracle by questioning men he knew to be wiser than he. Slowly, Socrates came to realize that men he once considered wise were often only pretending to know more than they did. And his tactic of questioning began what would come to be called the Socratic method, a way of learning through critical thinking. The Socratic method gave people a new way to think, but it ultimately ended Socrates's life. In 399 B.C., he was arrested and charged with corrupting the students of Athens with his blasphemous questions and famously condemned to death by drinking poison hemlock.

AMAZING ENGINEERS

∽ *Leading Ladies of STEM* ∽

For centuries, engineering was seen as a field for men only. And unfortunately, the stereotype persists: Only about 13 percent of engineers in the United States are female. But that didn't stop these tough, talented women. They chased their engineering dreams to rule the field.

Mother of Management: Lillian Gilbreth (1878–1972)

Lillian Gilbreth was a master of efficiency—as a mother of 12, she had to be! Drawing on her master's and doctorate degrees in psychology, she teamed up with her husband, Frank, to turn a scientific eye to managing household activities. The pair found faster and more efficient strategies for daily chores like washing dishes and brushing teeth. They turned this domestic talent into a career, studying ways for companies to motivate their workers and simplify their tasks. When Frank died suddenly in 1924, leaving Lillian with their large family to raise all on her own, she didn't falter. She continued their work, fearlessly balancing career and family at a time when that was a foreign concept to society. Along the way, she became the first female professor in the engineering school at Purdue University, in Indiana, U.S.A., and the first woman elected to the National Academy of Engineering.

Robot Revolutionary: Cynthia Breazeal (1967–)

Cynthia Breazeal has loved robots since age 10, when she watched *Star Wars* for the first time. She never lost her interest, studying robotics at the University of California at Santa Barbara and then at the Massachusetts Institute of Technology (MIT). But the more she learned, the more she wondered: Scientists had sent robots to the bottom of the ocean and even to Mars, so why weren't there robots in people's homes? In 2014, she started building Jibo, the world's first robot for families. Jibo can remember faces, take photos, tell you the weather, and crack jokes. Breazeal hopes it will soon also be able to give you recipes, read children's books out loud, and become a helpful part of the family.

Tech Leader:
Stephanie Hill (1965–)

Stephanie Hill didn't intend to become an engineer. Growing up, she loved math and thought she would pursue a career as an accountant. But while in college at the University of Maryland, Baltimore County, she took a class in computer programming and fell in love with the subject. As an African-American woman, she had few role models in her field to look up to; Hill rose to the very top anyway. She began her career with Lockheed Martin, the world's largest defense and technology company, in 1987. Today, she oversees business strategies and development opportunities of some of the world's most important discoveries and innovations in tech—from cybersecurity to space exploration—for the company. In 2017, Hill was named to *Black Enterprise* magazine's Most Powerful Executives in Corporate America list, and in 2014, she was named the U.S. Black Engineer of the Year by Career Communications Group and included on *Ebony* magazine's Power 100 list. She's passionate about sharing her love for engineering and encouraging students of all backgrounds to pursue science, technology, engineering, and math careers. "I believe that if you work very hard and treat people with respect, you can make a difference wherever you are, whoever you are," Hill says.

Video Game Visionary:
Kim Swift (1983–)

Video game designer Kim Swift thinks that toys aren't just for kids. She blew gamers away—and became one of the industry's brightest young superstars—when she released *Portal* in 2007. The game sent players on an adventure that broke the rules of physics, forcing them to rack their brains to renegotiate their relationship with the physical world as they rip open interconnected holes in space. Her second release was no less mind-bending: *Quantum Conundrum* required players to change the rule of physics—reversing gravity, slowing time, and entering something called "the fluffy dimension." Swift's work earned her a spot on *Forbes* magazine's 30 Under 30 list of young creators in 2012. And *Portal* is now part of the permanent collection at the Museum of Modern Art in New York City.

Grace Hopper

∽ Queen of Code ∽

When it comes to naming pioneers of computing, you can probably list a few of the most famous, such as Steve Jobs and Bill Gates. But you might have never even heard of Grace Hopper—one of the most influential computer scientists in history. In 2016, President Barack Obama posthumously awarded her the Presidential Medal of Freedom for her role in shaping modern technology.

When World War II broke out, Hopper was a 37-year-old professor teaching mathematics. Wanting to join the war effort, she tried to enlist in the Navy but failed the physical exam because—at five feet three inches (1.6 m) and 105 pounds (48 kg)—she was considered underweight. Instead, she joined the Navy Reserve and was assigned to a secret project at Harvard University, in Cambridge, Massachusetts. Hopper walked through the door and came face-to-face with Mark I, the world's first computer. The 51-foot (15-m)-tall machine looked impressive—but it didn't work. Hopper—who had earned both a master's degree and a Ph.D. in mathematics from Yale University—helped get Mark I functioning, and the computer spent the war solving equations that helped the military fight—and win.

After the war, Hopper hoped to stay and teach at Harvard, but the school did not hire female professors. So, in 1949, she went to work for the world's first computer start-up, Eckert-Mauchly Computer Corporation, as head of the software division. In those days, many small companies were making computers, but the machines all used their own languages and had no way of talking to one another. Hopper changed all that when she created a universal programming language. Called COBOL, it allowed everyone—not just mathematicians—to program computers. By the year 2000, 70 percent of all active code in the world was in COBOL.

> "You don't manage people; you manage things. You lead people."
> —*Grace Hopper*

Royal Rundown

BORN: December 9, 1906, New York, New York, U.S.A. **DIED:** January 1, 1992, Arlington, Virginia, U.S.A.
LED: Computer science **REMEMBERED FOR:** A universal computer programming language

Maryam Mirzakhani

❧ A Noble of Numbers ❧

For mathematicians, there is one award considered more distinguished than all others: the Fields Medal, often called the Nobel Prize of mathematics. But it could be argued the Fields Medal is even harder to win: It's awarded only every four years, and only to people age 40 or younger. When Maryam Mirzakhani won it in 2014, she became the first Iranian and the first and only woman ever to earn the honor.

Mirzakhani was born in Tehran, Iran, and attended an all-girls high school there. Though no girl had ever competed for Iran's International Mathematical Olympiad team, Mirzakhani did—and won gold medals in 1994 and 1995. After college, she left for the United States to attend graduate school at Harvard University. Early in life, she wanted to be a writer, but math won her over. "It is fun—it's like solving a puzzle or connecting the dots," she later said.

To non-mathematicians, Mirzakhani's work is difficult to wrap the mind around. She specialized in a field called hyperbolic geometry, which deals with extremely strange shapes: One might have the curvy surface of a Pringles potato chip but form a doughnut with multiple holes. If that's impossible to envision, don't worry—Mirzakhani's math dealt with shapes that don't exist in our three-dimensional world. She was also interested in a problem physicists have grappled with for decades: predicting how a set of billiard balls might move as they bounce around the table. Someday, Mirzakhani's work could impact real-life fields like cryptography, or code breaking. Sadly, Mirzakhani died of breast cancer at the age of 40, leaving behind a mourning mathematics world—and groundbreaking problems yet to be solved.

"The most rewarding part is the 'aha' moment, the excitement of discovery and enjoyment of understanding something new."
—Maryam Mirzakhani

Royal Rundown

❀ **BORN:** May 3, 1977, Tehran, Iran ❀ **DIED:** July 14, 2017, Palo Alto, California, U.S.A.
❀ **LED:** Mathematics ❀ **REMEMBERED FOR:** Advances in hyperbolic geometry

QUEENS
OF THE DEEP

⊷ *Leaders in Ocean Exploration* ⊷

The oceans cover more than 70 percent of Earth's surface. But we humans know so little about what's hiding beneath the waves that the sea has been called Earth's last frontier. Exploring the ocean takes bravery, smarts, and a driving curiosity. Luckily for science, the women on this page had all that and more.

Her Deepness:
Sylvia Earle (1935–)

Sylvia Earle has been the queen of ocean exploration for more than 40 years. Since her first dive at age 16, she has spent more than 7,000 hours (nearly a year in total!) underwater. In 1970, she led a group of five women scientists who lived in a capsule 1,250 feet (381 m) below the surface for a record-setting two weeks straight. Earle—nicknamed Her Deepness—has conducted groundbreaking research on algae, tracked marine mammals as they cross oceans, and discovered many new species of aquatic life. She was the first woman to be appointed chief scientist of the National Oceanic and Atmospheric Administration and was National Geographic's first female explorer-in-residence. Today, Earle devotes her time to raising awareness about the dire problems the ocean faces: floating patches of garbage the size of small countries, coral reefs that are rapidly disappearing, and overfishing that has reduced the populations of large fish like halibut and sharks.

First Lady of the Oceans:
Krystyna Chojnowska-Liskiewicz (1936–)

Krystyna Chojnowska-Liskiewicz always loved the ocean. Born in Warsaw, Poland, she earned a naval architecture degree and went to work as a ship designer. She went sailing every chance she got and even earned her captain's certificate. In March 1976, she set sail from Las Palmas, the capital of one of Spain's Canary Islands, in a 32-foot (9.8-m) yacht called the *Mazurek*, intending to become the first woman to sail solo around the world. The journey was harrowing: She weathered fierce storms in the South Atlantic, spent weeks with no radio contact, and had to pause her journey to be hospitalized for a severe kidney illness. But on April 21, 1978—more than two years after she had left—she sailed back into Las Palmas after circling the globe. "There were times when I thought I would never manage it," she said, but she did it anyway and achieved her goal of becoming the first woman to circle the globe solo.

Mapping Monarch: Marie Tharp (1920–2006)

In the 1940s, women were not allowed to join the crews of scientific research ships. But that didn't stop Marie Tharp from achieving her big dream: mapping the ocean floor. At that time, no one really knew what was hidden beneath the oceans. Using sonar pings from vessels crisscrossing the ocean, Tharp meticulously crunched the numbers at the desk in her office to create topographic maps revealing a hidden world beneath the waves. She discovered that there was a 10,000-mile (16,000-km)-long mountain chain and valley running down the middle of the ocean, in the North Atlantic. This discovery—called the Mid-Atlantic Ridge—was a crucial piece of evidence supporting the theory of plate tectonics, which explains how mountains, volcanoes, and earthquakes come to be. This helped us understand how our planet supports life and revolutionized the field of geology.

Admiral of Sea and Sky: Evelyn Fields (1949–)

The National Oceanic and Atmospheric Administration (NOAA) is the U.S. scientific agency in charge of keeping tabs on all the oceans, waterways, and atmosphere on Earth. It's a big job—but it wasn't too big for Evelyn Fields. In 1972, she became the first African-American woman to join the organization. As her first assignment, she boarded a survey vessel called *Mt. Mitchell* to chart the seas. It was just one of the many firsts Fields would go on to achieve in her career. In 1989, NOAA selected her to become the first woman to command a federal ship, a research vessel called the *McArthur*. One decade later, then president Bill Clinton selected her to serve as the director of NOAA Corps and Office of Marine and Aviation Operations—the first woman and the first African American to hold the position. She was also the first woman to reach the rank of rear admiral. Until her retirement in 2002, Fields oversaw a staff of hundreds, along with 15 research ships and 14 aircraft, together responsible for monitoring the health of all the world's water and air.

Sovereign of Sharks: Eugenie Clark (1922–2015)

Eugenie Clark learned to swim before the age of two—and that was just the beginning of a life she would spend in the water. Clark fell in love with the sea during her childhood visits to the New York Aquarium and studied ichthyology, the biology of fish, as she worked her way through Hunter College in the 1940s. Though there were few women in her field in the time after World War II—especially women of Japanese descent, like Clark—she quickly proved that women had a place in science. Clark's passion was sharks. Before she began researching them in the 1950s, sharks had a reputation as brainless killers. Clark spent her career fearlessly dispelling these myths, revealing that sharks are a complex, fascinating species who rarely bite humans—and then only when mistaking them for food. She discovered the first effective shark repellent: a natural secretion from a flatfish in the Red Sea. She dove into undersea caverns off Mexico's Yucatán Peninsula to find "sleeping sharks" drifting in water, proving the myth that sharks have to keep moving to breathe is false. For her pioneering work in the study of shark behavior and marine conservation, she earned the nickname Shark Lady.

Jill Tarter

∾ Alien Hunter ∾

Royal Rundown

❀ **BORN:** January 16, 1944, New York, U.S.A. ❀ **LEADS:** The search for alien life
❀ **KNOWN FOR:** Founding the SETI Institute and heading the search for extraterrestrial life

Are we alone? It's the question astronomer Jill Tarter has devoted her life to answering. As the co-founder and former director of the SETI (short for Search for ExtraTerrestrial Intelligence) Institute in Mountain View, California, U.S.A., Tarter has spent her career scanning the skies for signals from intelligent aliens.

What were you like as a kid?

I was a tomboy. I went camping and hunting and fishing with my dad as a young girl. I was always the only girl around, but I had a great time! My dad was interested in astronomy, and we spent many evenings walking on the beaches of Florida, where his family lived, and looking at the sky. But I didn't decide to become an astronomer until much later. I decided that I would be an engineer.

You grew up in the 1950s. What was it like trying to become an engineer at that time?

Back then, the only roles for women were as homemakers and mothers. When I told my high school counselors I wanted to take physics classes, they discouraged me. "Why do you want to take physics?" they asked. "You're just going to grow up and get married and have babies." But I powered through high school and was accepted to the engineering program at Cornell University in New York. When I walked into class the first day, I was shocked to discover that I was the only female in my entire class of 300!

How did you become interested in finding life on other planets?

At the end of graduate school, I had the opportunity to take a bunch of different courses just for fun. I took a course in star formation that totally blew me away. I had no idea that stars are born and that they die these dramatic deaths! I was hooked, so I switched to astronomy. One of my professors had a clever idea about how to use the university's telescope to look for artificial signals in space—the kind of signals intelligent life would send. I found the idea absolutely fascinating. For millennia, we had been asking priests or shamans what we should believe about life beyond Earth. But suddenly, we had tools that would allow us to actually find out the answer to this question. I thought that was something worth working on.

You've been searching for aliens for 50 years. Are you getting discouraged?

Think about it this way: Pretend that the universe is the same size as all the oceans on Earth. The area of space that we've searched in the past 50 years is only the equivalent of one 12-ounce glass! Now suppose that you were trying to find out if there were any fish in the ocean. Imagine you dumped that glass of water out and didn't see any fish. It would be a mistake to conclude the ocean has no fish! There's a lot more searching you could do—that's where we are today. And our tools, like telescopes and computers, are getting more powerful all the time. So, far from being discouraged, I'm really excited!

When do you think we will answer the question "Are we alone?"

I think we will find the answer during this century. That

Jill Tarter has spent her career watching and listening for signs of life elsewhere in the universe.

means a kid reading this right now could be the person to do it! Young people are going to see and perhaps even be part of teams that explore all these places in our solar system that could be home to life. We know there is water beneath the soil of Mars and oceans beneath the ice of Jupiter's moon Europa—and many more places besides. Scientists are planning missions to these places right now. I would love to be 10 years old right now so I could be part of the discoveries!

Signals From Space
How Jill Tarter Hunts for Aliens

Jill Tarter and other alien-hunting scientists started out using radio signals to look for life on other planets. Using giant radio dishes, they listen to sounds coming our way from different parts of the galaxy. Most of these radio signals are white noise created by stars and planets, but certain signals can be produced only by technology. Usually, we just hear signals made by our own satellites or cell phones. But someday, we might stumble upon one of these signals that isn't coming from Earth. That would mean intelligent life is out there! More recently, scientists have started listening for other kinds of signals, too—like optical signals sent by lasers from another planet. Humans used to have to painstakingly analyze telescope data to hunt for these signals, but now computers are learning to look for patterns much better and faster than people can.

QUEENS OF INDUSTRY

❦ *Boss Businesswomen* ❦

It takes guts and grit to hike a mountain. It takes those same qualities to climb to the top of the business world. These entrepreneurs and CEOs worked their way up—concocting creams in their kitchens and even cruising around for trash—to become some of the most successful women in the world.

Ruler of YouTube:
Susan Wojcicki (1958–)

During college, Susan Wojcicki took a summer job at a technology start-up—as the receptionist. She thought what was going on around her was thrilling, and she knew she wanted to help build companies like that one. So Wojcicki started taking computer science classes and earned master's degrees in economics and business. Then, in 1998, Wojcicki and her husband rented out their garage to some Stanford University graduates starting a company. That company was Google, and in 1999, Wojcicki would join on as its first marketing employee. She went on to become Google's senior vice president of advertising and commerce, responsible for 95 percent of the company's earnings. In 2006, she led the company's purchase of YouTube, and today she is YouTube's CEO. Called "the most powerful woman on the Internet" by *Time* magazine, Wojcicki uses that power to speak out against gender discrimination at tech companies and inspire girls to become interested in computer science.

Queen of Clean: Linda Cobb (1950–)

Today, Linda Cobb is known as the Queen of Clean, a best-selling author, national speaker, and television personality who shares clever cleaning tips with a side of humor. But Linda's life wasn't always sparkling. When she was in her mid-30s, Cobb's husband and their child passed away. She was rocked to the core, but she pulled herself out of her grief and pain to try to go on with her life. In 1982, she found a job as a scheduling coordinator for Moretz Cleaning in Marysville, Michigan, U.S.A. Cobb learned the secrets of how to clean up everything from kitchen floors to water damage. She became partners with the owners, and in 1991, she bought out the company. Friends suggested that she write a newsletter about her cleaning secrets, and Cobb began appearing on radio shows, then TV shows—first appearing on *Good Morning America* in 1997. She was terrified of public appearances at first, but she pushed through her fear. Today, Cobb is famous, beloved for her witty personality and her oddball cleaning methods, which include scrubbing wood floors with tea bags and toilets with powdered drink mix.

Queen of Hidden Treasure:
Zhang Yin (1957–)

You've heard the expression "turning trash into treasure"? Zhang Yin literally did it! In 2002, she and her husband could be found driving across the United States in a used minivan, asking garbage dumps to give them their paper scraps. The dumps were eager to hand over the trash. But where they saw waste, Yin saw wealth: She knew that paper could be collected, shipped to China, and recycled into cardboard. There, it could be used to make boxes packed with goods—which could be shipped right back to America, dumped, and collected by Yin once again. Her company, Nine Dragons Paper, is now worth billions. In 2006, Yin became both the first woman to top the list of richest people in China and also one of the wealthiest self-made women in the world.

Makeup Monarch:
Estée Lauder (1908–2004)

A master of appearance, Estée Lauder misled the media for years about her life story, saying she was a European countess. Later, she revealed that she wasn't royalty: She was actually the daughter of working-class Jewish immigrants. But by then, she had already begun her reign as the queen of cosmetics. She got her start in beauty at a young age, helping her chemist uncle mix up skin-care creams for his small business in the family kitchen in Queens, New York. Lauder refined and improved the products and started selling them on her own. She had no money for advertising, so she made up for it with smart selling strategies. She gave free demonstrations at beauty salons and came up with the "gift with purchase" deal that most cosmetics brands have come to use. By the early 1950s, her line was a regular feature at high-end department stores across America. She retired with an estimated five billion dollars.

Queens of the Stone Age

∾ Archaeological Aristocrats ∾

Extraordinary archaeological finds can change what we know about humankind's earliest ancestors. These ancient women were among the most groundbreaking discoveries ever.

Fundamental Find:
Lucy

When Lucy was discovered, in 1974 in Ethiopia, she was the most complete early human skeleton ever found. At 3.2 million years old, Lucy helped experts understand how humans first began to split from the ancient ancestor we share with apes. Like an ape, Lucy—a member of the human species *Australopithecus afarensis*—had a small brain and petite frame: At just 3.5 feet (1.1 m) tall, she was the same height as a modern five-year-old child. And like an ape, she had strong, muscular legs and grasping feet, showing that she probably spent time in trees. But scientists can tell from her joints that Lucy walked on two legs—just like we do. And her teeth show that, unlike a chimp, she wasn't just eating tree fruit but also food she found on the savanna, like grasses and maybe even meat. But Lucy's bones still haven't given up all their secrets. Even today, scientists are unraveling mysteries about what her life was like, and whether she was a direct ancestor of *Homo sapiens*—us.

The Beginning of Us:
Ardi

Experts thought Lucy was the oldest early human ever discovered—until they found Ardi's crushed skeleton in 2009 in an area of Ethiopia near where Lucy was located. When scientists dated Ardi's bones, they discovered they were shockingly old—around 4.4 million years! Scientists estimate that Ardi (short for her species name, *Ardipithecus ramidus*) stood four feet (1.2 m) tall and weighed 110 pounds (50 kg). Though she looked very apelike, she had a few traits that hinted she could be an ancient ancestor of humans, including small, humanlike canine teeth and dexterous hands that might have been good at catching things and carrying them. While chimps used their large canines to intimidate each other and assert their social status, Ardi's small chompers show that—like modern people—her species may have had to figure out other ways to get along.

Facing the Past: Wilma

The Neanderthals were our closest pre-historic relatives. For 200,000 years, they dominated Earth, living in every corner of Europe and parts of Asia. Then, about 40,000 years ago, they disappeared. In 2008, for the very first time, scientists used measurements of previously discovered Neanderthal fossils and extracted DNA that was surviving in 43,000 bones to come up with a model of what one Neanderthal woman might have looked like. Named Wilma, she had red hair, light skin, and freckles. Wilma may have hunted large animals like horses, bison, and deer—dangerous work, judging by the healed fractures found on Neanderthal arms and skulls. She lived with her Neanderthal family in limestone caves. Together, they cared for their sick, used stone tools, and buried their dead. No one knows exactly why this ancient yet smart and sophisticated people died out—but Wilma puts a face to the mystery.

Ancient Artists: Cave Painters

Were women the world's first artists? On September 12, 1940, four teenagers were exploring the woods in the southwest of France when they stumbled upon a hole in the ground. Recalling a local legend about a secret tunnel that led to buried treasure, the kids dropped down the narrow shaft into a cave. What they found there was indeed a priceless treasure—it just wasn't the kind they were expecting. The walls in the Lascaux cave system were covered with horses, deer, and many animals that are now extinct: aurochs, woolly rhinos, and cave hyenas. Archaeologists later determined that the paintings were about 15,000 years old. Since then, many other cave paintings have been found all over the world, including hand stencils made by blowing pigment against a hand held against the wall. But who were these ancient artists? A 2013 study analyzed the hand size of the stencils used in eight cave paintings in France and Spain and found something surprising: About three-quarters of them appear to have belonged to females.

QUEENS OF SPACE

~ *Rulers of the Universe* ~

No boundary in this world—or beyond—could stop the superior scientists on these pages. More brilliant than the stars they studied, these women blasted off into space science and never looked down.

Sovereign of the Stars:
Annie Jump Cannon (1863–1941)

Everyone has looked up at the night sky and wondered how many stars are up there. For Annie Jump Cannon, answering that question became her life's work. Born in 1863, Cannon studied physics and astronomy at Wellesley College, one of the top schools for women at the time. But despite her education, there were very few jobs open to her as a female. The only astronomy work she could find was as a human "computer," whose job was to look over photographs of the night sky and compare the positions of stars. It was tedious and paid only 50 cents an hour. But Cannon proved to be a genius at analyzing stars and classifying them by temperature. Between 1911 and 1915, she classified 5,000 stars a month and developed a system—still in use today—for ranking stars as O, B, A, F, G, K, or M, with O being the hottest and M the coolest. She classified more than 350,000 stars in her lifetime and helped shape modern astronomy into what it is today.

Ruler of Sea and Sky:
Kathryn Sullivan (1951–)

On October 11, 1984, a female American astronaut stepped outside a spacecraft for the very first time. She was Kathryn Sullivan. And though her most famous moment happened high above the surface of Earth, Sullivan actually got her start at the bottom of the ocean, when she studied the seafloor after earning her doctorate in geology. In 1978, Sullivan took a break from diving below the waves to soar up into space when NASA selected her to be an astronaut. As one of six women in the first astronaut class to include both genders, Sullivan faced resistance from men who didn't want to share the shuttle. But she proved she was more than capable when she and co-astronaut David Leetsma donned space suits and left the safety of the craft to demonstrate that satellites could be refueled in orbit. After two more spaceflights, Sullivan combined her loves of sea and sky and became chief scientist, and later, deputy administrator, of the National Oceanic and Atmospheric Administration.

Queen of the Solar System:
Claudia Alexander (1959–2015)

In a field where nearly everyone was a white man, Claudia Alexander stood out. But not only because she was a black woman: Alexander was a brilliant scientist who changed what we know about our solar system and a leader whose love of learning inspired everyone around her. After a high school internship with NASA that fostered her love of space science and a 1993 doctorate in plasma physics from the University of Michigan, she joined NASA's Galileo mission to study Jupiter. With Alexander at the helm, the mission discovered 21 moons, revealed Jupiter's atmosphere for the first time, and discovered an atmosphere on the moon Ganymede. Alexander also worked on the European Space Agency's Rosetta mission, a 10-year project to study and land on a comet, which it did in 2014. She shared her infectious love for her work, writing not only scientific papers but also children's books and science fiction.

Empress of Exoplanets:
Debra Fischer (1953–)

Thirty years ago, astronomers didn't know of a single planet outside our solar system; nobody had any idea whether ours was the only place in the universe where planets orbited a sun. Now, thanks to astronomer Debra Fischer and her colleagues, we know that space is teeming with planets orbiting distant stars. They have discovered thousands of these otherworldly worlds, called exoplanets, and now new ones are revealed almost every week. Fischer—who was finishing graduate school just as the first exoplanet was discovered in 1992—became one of the very first planet hunters. In 1999, she discovered the first star system outside our solar system that has multiple planets: Upsilon Andromedae, where three giant gas planets orbit their sun. Since then, Fischer has helped discover all kinds of weird and wild worlds, including one that has two suns—just like the fictional *Star Wars* planet Tatooine.

Mildred Benson

∞ Private Eye Princess ∞

"I have solved some mysteries, I'll admit, and I enjoy it, but I'm sure there are many other girls who could do the same."
—*Nancy Drew*

In 1930, a new kind of heroine appeared on the scene. The teenage girl detective was bold enough to speak her mind and brave enough to chase down any mystery that came her way. She was Nancy Drew, the starring character of detective novels for young adults that have sold more than 70 million copies. Many women list her as their childhood inspiration, including Supreme Court justice Sonia Sotomayor (p. 63) and former secretary of state Hillary Clinton.

The plucky girl detective is one of the most famous characters in history. But few know the story of the woman behind Nancy Drew: Mildred Benson. Though dozens of authors penned Nancy Drew tales under the pen name of Carolyn Keene, Benson wrote 23 of the first 30 books and gave Nancy the qualities that make her still famous today: intelligence, self-reliance, and determination.

In the 1940s, while working on the Nancy Drew series, Benson took another job as a court reporter for the *Toledo Times*. She became notorious for her habit of waiting outside councilmen's office doors to force them into an interview. As the story goes, one got so desperate to avoid her that he climbed out his office window. When she wasn't writing, Benson swam, flew planes, and trekked through the Central American jungle to visit Maya ruins and archaeological dig sites—much like her adventuring character Nancy Drew.

In a time when many girls were encouraged to marry young and spend their lives as housewives, bold and brave Nancy was a role model. "She was ahead of her time," Benson once said. "She was not typical. She was what the girls were ready for and were aspiring for, but had not achieved."

Royal Rundown

✿ **BORN:** July 10, 1905, Ladora, Iowa, U.S.A. ✿ **DIED:** May 28, 2002, Toledo, Ohio, U.S.A.
✿ **LED:** Detective stories ✿ **REMEMBERED FOR:** Breaking the mold of what a girl could be

Agatha Christie

❧ Queen of Crime ❧

A group of people are gathered together in a country house or on a train stuck in the snow when—oh no!—a body is discovered. There's been a murder ... but who committed the crime? As the mystery unravels, heinous plots and undercover acts are revealed until, finally, the culprit is revealed. If this story sounds familiar, that's because it's been the basic plot of most detective tales for the past 50 years. For that we can thank Agatha Christie, the pioneering author who invented the modern detective narrative, earning her the nickname the Queen of Crime.

Christie was born in 1890, the youngest of three siblings, in southwest England. She was painfully shy and had no playmates: Her brother and sister, Monty and Madge, were more than a decade older. So when she was bored, Christie would pass the time making up stories. Her mother, who educated the children at home, encouraged her to write them down. By age 17, Christie had written many short stories and one novel; by 21, she had written what would go on to become her first published book: *The Mysterious Affair at Styles*.

Over her 56-year writing career, Christie created two famous detectives—Hercule Poirot and Jane Marple—and invented the "whodunit," where the reader tries to guess who the culprit is before the author reveals it at the end of the book. The format proved irresistible: Christie would go on to write 66 detective novels distributed in 45 languages. Her books have sold more than two billion copies worldwide, making her not only the world's best-selling detective writer but also the most-read novelist in history.

> "Very few of us are what we seem."
> —*Agatha Christie*

👑 Royal Rundown

- 👑 **BORN:** September 15, 1890, Torquay, U.K.
- 👑 **DIED:** January 12, 1976, Winterbrook, U.K.
- 👑 **LED:** Crime novels
- 👑 **REMEMBERED FOR:** Inventing the "whodunit"

145

Nobel Nobles

The Nobel Prize is the world's most prestigious award. Each year, six are given out internationally in the fields of physics, chemistry, medicine or physiology, literature, and economics, and for the promotion of worldwide peace. Here are some of history's most outstanding female Nobel winners.

1931:
Jane Addams

A member of the first generation of college-educated women in the United States, Jane Addams bucked the social standards of her time and devoted her life to social work instead of becoming a wife and mother. In 1889, Addams, along with a friend named Ellen Gates Starr, moved into an old mansion in a neighborhood of immigrants in Chicago, Illinois, U.S.A. There, she listened to the needs of the locals and in response founded a nursery, a kindergarten, a playground, a gymnasium, and affordable housing in a residence. She lived there for the rest of her life, advocating for causes she believed in, such as labor unions, safe working conditions, and abolishing child labor. In 1931, Addams became the first American woman to win the Nobel Peace Prize.

1903:
Marie Curie

Today, women hold less than 24 percent of science and technology jobs; back in the early 1900s, there were almost no females in those fields. Yet, with no mentors to pave the way and facing great obstacles, Marie Curie became one of the greatest scientists the world has ever seen. For her research on radioactivity and discovering the elements radium and polonium, she won not just one, but two Nobel Prizes. She was the first woman ever to win a Nobel, and the first person in history—male or female—to win two.

1993: Toni Morrison

When Toni Morrison was a kid, she loved to listen to her father's stories about African-American history and culture. When she grew up, she became famous for telling her versions of those same stories. Beginning in 1970 with *The Bluest Eye*, she penned novels that brought the African-American experience to life with complex characters and rich language. Her 1987 book, *Beloved*, secured her spot in the history books and earned her several literary awards. Five years later, her work earned her the 1993 Nobel Prize in literature—making her the first African American to earn the honor.

2015: Tu Youyou

Tu Youyou won the Nobel Prize in medicine in 2015 ... and she doesn't have a medical degree or a doctorate! After attending pharmacology school in Beijing, China, Youyou joined a secret government research team searching for a cure for malaria. When she started, more than 240,000 compounds around the world had already been tested and failed. But in a book about ancient Chinese medicine, Youyou found a reference to a substance called sweet wormwood that had been used to treat malaria around A.D. 400. It was a success! The treatment has since saved millions of lives—and made Youyou China's first Nobel laureate.

1983: Barbara McClintock

While in graduate school at Cornell University, Barbara McClintock began to peer very closely at corn, studying its chromosomes, or molecules that carry a cell's genetic material. In the 1940s, she discovered something brand-new: that genes can move around within their chromosomes, "jumping" from one spot to another. McClintock believed this gave organisms a way to adapt quickly to changes in their environments. She was right, but scientists scoffed at her for decades, until DNA was discovered in the 1960s. In 1983, she won the Nobel Prize in medicine.

Chapter Eight

QUEENS OF ADVENTURE

Some queens don't lead nations. Instead, they lead the charge, rule their field, or champion their convictions. By plane, by train, and on foot, some journeyed to the farthest reaches of the globe. Others worked their way to the pinnacle of their profession, used their smarts to save lives, or brought their cause to the forefront of the world's consciousness. The bold, brave women in these pages are pioneers and earthshakers who were not afraid to take on a challenge.

Eliza Scidmore

～ Travel Queen ～

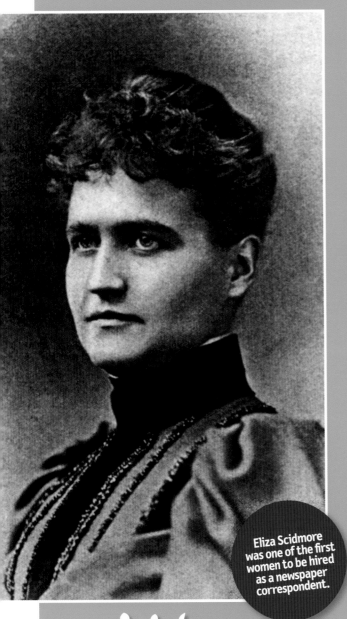

Eliza Scidmore was one of the first women to be hired as a newspaper correspondent.

I t was 1883, and Eliza Scidmore decided she had had enough of her ordinary life. Tired of writing society columns for newspapers around the United States, she took the money she had saved from her work and bought a ticket on a steamship headed to Alaska. Few Americans had seen the frozen northern land, and Scidmore wanted to be one of the first. It was the beginning of a long life she would spend traveling to faraway places and documenting what she found there for the rest of the world.

A TASTE FOR ADVENTURE

Eliza Scidmore (SID-more) was a born adventurer. As a child, she studied maps and geography and dreamed of traveling to exotic corners of the globe. After attending Ohio's Oberlin College for a few semesters, Scidmore left to pursue a career. At the time, the work culture was shifting; women were beginning to be hired by newspapers, and Scidmore wanted to try her hand at journalism. She became very successful at writing society columns, earning $1,000 (the equivalent of $26,000 in today's money) in a single week in the 1880s. But the work wasn't enough for Scidmore. She wanted to see the world—and now she had the funds to do it.

In 1883, Scidmore boarded the steamship *Idaho* and traveled to Alaska. She saw a tidewater glacier flowing down to the ocean and cracking off into huge icebergs. She met native Tlingit people. And when the *Idaho* went off course, she and her fellow passengers became the first tourists to visit Glacier Bay, now a national park and World Heritage site. Scidmore wrote about her Alaska adventures and published them as a book—the first comprehensive travelogue of the region.

Royal Rundown

❀ **BORN:** October 14, 1856, Madison, Wisconsin, U.S.A. ❀ **DIED:** November 3, 1928, Geneva, Switzerland
❀ **LED:** The American wilderness ❀ **REMEMBERED FOR:** Becoming *National Geographic* magazine's first official female writer, photographer, and board member, and bringing Japanese cherry blossoms to the nation's capital

TRAVEL PIONEER

Now an established travel writer, Scidmore set her sights on a new adventure: venturing to East Asia. In 1885, she journeyed to Japan, which had recently opened up to Western visitors. Scidmore fell in love with the country, writing dispatches about everything from Japanese tea ceremonies to silkworm farms. And in what would become her most famous act, she returned to Washington, D.C., with photographs of Japan's blooming cherry trees—and began trying to persuade President Grover Cleveland to plant the trees along the Tidal Basin, a reservoir in Washington, D.C. Today, the trees are one of the capital's most famous attractions.

In 1888, Scidmore joined the brand-new National Geographic Society, founded "for the increase and diffusion of geographical knowledge." One of just 12 female members out of 200, she was admired by the magazine's first president and editor, who sought her advice about developing the magazine. Scidmore quickly became a respected part of the organization, as both a board member and the society's first female writer and photographer. She brought in explorers and diplomats to lecture and gave her own talks on Asia and Alaska. In the early 1900s, she again left for Asia—this time with a camera in hand. She documented her travels across India, Japan, China, and the island of Java and published the photographs and essays in *National Geographic* magazine. In 1914, she published the magazine's first color photographs, tinted by hand.

LASTING LEGACY

Scidmore returned to her beloved Japan many times through the years. Her accounts of the landscape and people exposed curious Westerners to a whole different part of the world. When Scidmore died in 1928, her ashes were buried in Yokohama, Japan. As time passed, Scidmore slipped into obscurity, and few people today have heard of her. But a reminder of her appears every spring, when the thousands of cherry trees she helped bring to the nation's capital burst into bloom.

Scidmore spent years trying to bring Japan's beautiful blossoms to the United States. In 1912, more than 3,000 cherry trees were planted along the Tidal Basin in Washington, D.C.

COMMANDING KINGS

King of the Wilderness

John Muir (1838–1914)

After nearly losing his sight in a factory accident as a young man, John Muir resolved to spend his life admiring the beauty of the natural world. He moved out West, far from industrial America, and spent years hiking in and around the future site of Yosemite National Park—an education he called the "University of the Wilderness." Muir began publishing articles and essays urging people to be more responsible with America's land. He was one of the first people to pioneer the idea of creating protected areas to keep the wild lands wild. Muir personally led President Theodore Roosevelt around places that went on to become protected parks, like Yosemite. He also formed the Sierra Club, an environmental group dedicated to the preservation of America's natural beauty for future generations of campers, hikers, and explorers.

151

QUEENS OF THE WILDERNESS

❧ *True Trailblazers* ❧

No location was too remote for these adventuring women. They traversed mountain passes, snowy peaks, and dark forests, all on a mission to see the world. Some broke the rules. Others broke records. All were masters of the great outdoors.

First Female National Park Ranger:
Clare Marie Hodges (1890–1970)

In the summer of 1918, many of America's able-bodied men were overseas fighting World War I. Women became factory workers and police officers—but there weren't any female park rangers. That is, until Clare Marie Hodges. Hodges had first visited Yosemite National Park at the age of 14, arriving there after a four-day journey on horseback. She fell in love with the valley's beauty and returned in 1916 to teach at a nearby school. She spent her free time learning the trails by heart, eventually talking her way into a job there in 1918. For the next 30 years, she was the only female park ranger in America. Hodges had the same responsibilities as male rangers and wore a similar uniform—complete with a badge and a Stetson hat.

Tough Traveler:
Isabella Bird (1831–1904)

In the Victorian age, few British women left their houses unescorted—let alone traveled the world solo. But Isabella Bird didn't care about society's norms: She craved adventure. Bird caught the travel bug on her first sea voyage, to America in 1854, which was recommended by her doctors as a treatment for her insomnia and depression. After that, she climbed Hawaii's highest volcanic peaks, rode through a blizzard in the Rocky Mountains with her eyes frozen shut, and went on an 8,000-mile (12,875-km) journey through China. She became a travel writer at age 44 and a photographer at age 60, documenting her bold adventures for a fascinated audience back home.

Founder of the Girl Scouts:
Juliette Gordon Low (1860–1927)

In 1912, after she met Sir Robert Baden-Powell, the founder of the Boy Scouts, an inspired Juliette Gordon Low telephoned her cousin. "I've got something for the girls of Savannah, and all of America, and all the world, and we're going to start it tonight!" the Georgia native said. That "something" was the Girl Scouts. The first troops were known as Girl Guides, made up of girls who showed up in their brothers' Boy Scout uniforms, eager to learn the same skills the boys were taught. They loved the experience so much that Low devoted her life—and her life savings—to the project. Today, the Girl Scouts is the largest educational organization for girls in the world, with about 2.5 million current members.

Heroic Hiker:
Grandma Gatewood (1887–1973)

She was the first woman to hike the entire 2,050-mile (3,299-km) Appalachian Trail by herself. And she did it at age 67, as a mother of 11 and grandmother of 23! Emma "Grandma" Gatewood had survived more than 30 years in an abusive marriage when she decided enough was enough. She put on her sneakers, stuffed a blanket and a plastic shower curtain in a knapsack to protect her from the elements, and took off. With no sleeping bag, tent, or compass, she hiked from May to September of 1955,

sleeping under picnic tables and eating canned sausages, raisins, peanut butter, and greens she found on the trail. One hundred forty-six days and six pairs of shoes later, she made it. She went on to hike the trail three times total (the first person ever to do so) and help establish the 1,444-mile (2,324-km) Buckeye Trail in her home state of Ohio.

Globe-trotting Gal:
Ida Pfeiffer (1797–1858)

Until she was 45 years old, Ida Pfeiffer led a normal 19th-century life: She got married, had children, and stayed home taking care of them. But after her husband died and her children grew up and left home, Pfeiffer found herself suddenly free to do whatever she wanted. And she wanted to see the world. At the time, it was considered improper for women to travel for fun. So Pfeiffer told everyone around her that she was going on a religious pilgrimage to Jerusalem. En route, she toured most of the Middle East. When she got back, she published a best-selling—but anonymous—travel diary, which funded more trips. She rode camels in the Middle East's Fertile Crescent, went on tiger hunts in India, and observed the culture of the Batak people of Indonesia, who sometimes practiced cannibalism. By the time she died, she had traveled more than 170,000 miles (273,588 km)—in a time before airplanes or even trains were built for comfort.

Bessie Coleman

❧ Flying Queen ❧

"I refused to take no for an answer."
—Bessie Coleman

I n 1922, a crowd gathered on a New York airfield was treated to an aerial spectacle. A small biplane swooped across the sky, performing stunts like barrel rolls and figure eights. Even more astonishing was the pilot who stepped from the craft after it landed: a woman of African and Native American descent named Bessie Coleman.

At the time, neither women nor people of color were allowed to fly. But Coleman wasn't the type to be deterred by unjust rules. As a child, she had walked miles to attend school, where she had discovered her talent for math. On the side, she worked as a laundress, saving up the money she earned to finance her education at the Colored Agricultural and Normal University in Oklahoma, now called Langston University. After hearing the stories of brave pilots in World War I, Coleman decided she'd like to fly herself. She applied to schools in the United States—but was rejected because of her gender and skin color. So she packed up and moved to France, where women were allowed to fly. She earned her license from the Fédération Aéronautique Internationale in 1921—two years before famous flier Amelia Earhart earned hers.

Coleman took to the skies as a professional stunt pilot. Crowds paid to watch her loop, spin, and dive above their heads. Coleman flew all kinds of craft, from tiny biplanes to planes left over from World War I. She traveled all around the United States to lecture on aviation. And she used her newfound celebrity to fight racism, forcing promoters of her stunt shows to do away with segregated audience entrances. When Coleman died in a flying accident at the age of 34, the world lost an icon and an inspiration for generations of pilots who would follow her.

BLACK HERITAGE
USA 32
BESSIE COLEMAN

👑 Royal Rundown

❀ **BORN:** January 26, 1892, Atlanta, Texas, U.S.A. ❀ **DIED:** April 30, 1926, Jacksonville, Florida, U.S.A.
❀ **LED:** Air shows ❀ **REMEMBERED FOR:** Breaking barriers to become the first female African-American pilot

Elsie MacGill

❧ Hurricane Queen ❧

Near the start of World War II, the German military had invaded much of Western Europe, and it looked as though England could be next. It would be the job of the British Royal Air Force to defend the island nation against the deadly Nazi Luftwaffe (air force)—but they didn't have enough planes to meet the challenge. The job to produce more fell to Canadian Car and Foundry, a small company in Ontario, Canada, that manufactured railway cars. It was Elsie MacGill's job to turn it into a fighter plane factory.

MacGill was no stranger to tough challenges. In 1929, on the morning she was to graduate from the University of Michigan with a master's degree in aeronautical engineering, she woke up paralyzed from the waist down: She had been struck with polio. But she didn't let go of her dream. For the next three years, MacGill wrote articles on aviation until she had regained the strength to walk with the aid of two metal walking sticks. She took an engineering job and—already the first Canadian woman to receive a bachelor's degree in electrical engineering and the first woman anywhere to earn a master's degree in aeronautical engineering—she became the first practicing female engineer in Canada and the first woman in the world to design an aircraft. As chief aeronautical engineer at Canadian Car and Foundry, she overhauled the production line, expanded the workforce, and started pumping out Hawker Hurricane fighter planes for the British. These aircraft would go on to be an essential part of the war effort.

MacGill's Maple Leaf II biplane was the world's first aircraft fully designed by a woman.

Royal Rundown

❀ **BORN:** March 27, 1905, Vancouver, British Columbia, Canada ❀ **DIED:** November 4, 1980, Cambridge, Massachusetts, U.S.A.
❀ **LED:** Aeronautical engineering ❀ **REMEMBERED FOR:** Becoming the world's first female aeronautical engineer

Biruté Mary Galdikas

⚜ Queen of the Orangutans ⚜

> "The tropical rainforest is the most complex thing an ordinary human can experience on this planet."
> —*Biruté Mary Galdikas*

Before Biruté Mary Galdikas came along, orangutans were a mystery to the world. Many scientists believed that the shy and solitary creatures, which live deep in the forests of Borneo and Sumatra, were impossible to study. But Galdikas proved them wrong. She spent years trekking through jungles to become the world's foremost authority on these elusive animals—and their greatest champion in the fight against extinction.

CURIOUS GIRL

Paleontologist Louis Leakey famously recruited three women to study great apes. Two of the most well known are Jane Goodall, the first person to discover that chimpanzees use tools, and Dian Fossey, who lived among gorillas in Rwanda, Africa, until she was killed in 1985. But not as many people have heard of the third woman: Biruté Mary Galdikas, who to this day spends most of her time in Borneo rehabilitating orangutans.

It all started when six-year-old Galdikas checked out her first library book: *Curious George.* Inspired by the story of man and monkey, Galdikas decided that she wanted to become an explorer. She studied first in Canada and then the United States when her family immigrated there in 1964, earning degrees in psychology, zoology, and anthropology. As a graduate

Royal Rundown

❀ **BORN:** May 10, 1946, Wiesbaden, Germany
❀ **LEADS:** Primatology ❀ **KNOWN FOR:** A safer world for orangutans

Galdikas among the orangutans in the Bornean rainforest

student at the University of California, Los Angeles, she went to a lecture given by Louis Leakey, the legendary scientist who had discovered the remains of humankind's earliest ancestors in East Africa. After the lecture, Galdikas waited until she was the last person left in the audience, then approached Leakey with her question. "I want to study orangutans," she said. "Will you help me?" Impressed with her passion, Leakey raised the money to launch the project.

INTO THE JUNGLE

When it came time to leave for the rainforest, Galdikas was nervous. She was intimidated by Goodall and Fossey, who were already successfully studying great apes. When Galdikas arrived in Borneo in October 1971, she was just 25 years old. The abandoned hut she was to live in was filthy. To find orangutans, she had to trek through black river water up to her armpits as leeches attached themselves to her neck. Most days, she saw no signs of the animals.

After months of difficult, exhausting work, Galdikas finally started figuring out how to find and track the orangutans. She was the first scientist to observe all kinds of orangutan behavior: fighting, mating, and giving birth. She realized that though orangutans are solitary creatures, they're not loners: They use complex calls to keep track of each other in the forest, and they come together to compete for mates and access to food.

SAVING A SPECIES

As Galdikas discovered how orangutans lived, she also learned they were in great danger. There are three orangutan species that exist only on the island of Borneo (shared between Indonesia, Brunei, and Malaysia) and the island of Sumatra. Logging is destroying the forests they rely on, and some people hunt orangutans for food or capture them to keep as pets. Galdikas began taking in captive orangutans, rehabilitating them, and returning them to the wild. It wasn't easy—the animals, which can weigh as much as 300 pounds (136 kg) would rip up her books and clothing and drink her shampoo and toothpaste. But that didn't stop Galdikas, who had made helping orangutans her life's mission.

In the decades since she first entered the Bornean rainforest, Galdikas has become these animals' biggest champion. She has lobbied the Indonesian government to set aside parks for orangutans to live in safely and returned hundreds of the animals to the wild. It's a tough battle: There are estimates that there were more than 230,000 orangutans a century ago, but today, according to Galdikas's organization, Orangutan Foundation International, there are only about 80,000 orangutans left. For Galdikas, these intelligent, gentle animals are worth fighting for.

COMMANDING KINGS

King of Human Evolution

Louis Leakey (1903–1972)

Where do we come from? It's a question that has fascinated humans for thousands of years, and it was the life's work of Louis Leakey. A paleoanthropologist—a scientist who studies human fossils—he brought the study of human origins into the public eye. Born in Kenya, Africa, to missionary parents, Leakey found his first artifacts—ancient stone tools—as a teenager. That discovery helped convince him that Africa was the birthplace of humankind, a notion that most people at the time didn't think was true. But Leakey made proving it his mission. Along the way, he teamed up with his archaeologist wife, Mary Leakey, and the two made one incredible discovery after another: One of their most famous was early fossils of an ancient species of human, *Homo habilis*, which walked across Africa about two million years ago.

Conservation Crusaders

The World's First All-Female
∽ Anti-Poaching Squad ∽

The Black Mambas prepare for night patrols.

Africa is home to some of the world's most incredible animals. Lions, elephants, mountain gorillas, and black rhinos roam the forests and savannas. Tourists from all over the world flock to catch a glimpse of these rare creatures in their natural habitats. But they're not the only ones on the lookout for wildlife: So are poachers, criminals who illegally hunt animals so that their body parts—such as tusks, pelts, or bones—can be sold for huge sums of money. At the rate they are currently being killed by poachers, some African animals could go extinct within our lifetimes.

It's a tough problem. Luckily, South Africa has a tough team to fight back. Meet the Black Mambas, a squad of highly trained, camo-clad women who patrol Balule Nature Reserve in South Africa's Krueger National Park and guard the planet's most precious wildlife. They are the world's first all-female anti-poaching squad.

A WAR WITHOUT WEAPONS

Many anti-poaching units are made up of men who are heavily armed with military weapons and use high-tech

The Black Mambas perform routine patrols to guard the wildlife against poachers.

tools like helicopters to ambush poachers in the act. But the Black Mambas—named for Africa's fearsome snake—have a different tactic: They believe they can deter the bad guys without violence. Their only weapons are pepper spray and handcuffs. And their success has ushered in new ideas about what it takes to save Africa's animals.

Mambas must go through months of intense training, learning how to move through the bush without being seen and how to survive alone in the wilderness. Once they're official rangers, they spend three weeks at a time on duty, patrolling the park on foot and by jeep. Experts in observation, they search for human tracks, holes in fencing, and other signs of break-ins. They find and dismantle poachers' camps and traps they have set. They assist trapped and injured animals. If they come face-to-face with a poacher in the bush, they can use walkie-talkies to call for backup. But often, help is too far away to answer—meaning that this isn't a job for the faint of heart.

A NEW PRESENCE

Angry poachers can be dangerous, but they're not the only things the Mambas need to watch out for: Animals can attack, too. Mambas have been charged by elephants and surrounded by lions. But the rangers are highly skilled, and so far, no one has died on the job.

Female rangers are still rare in South Africa. When the Mambas first started, in 2013, they were laughed at. But their success speaks for itself: Poaching in the parks is down by more than 70 percent—and people are no longer laughing. Opinions have changed, and many consider the Mambas local heroes. In a society where women are usually expected to stay at home, joining the Mambas provides women with a job and way to earn for their families. Every year, the group's numbers grow.

FACING THE FUTURE

The Mambas have also become role models for local kids. In the Black Mambas Bush Babies program, schoolchildren between the ages of 12 and 15 learn about local wildlife and how to protect it. They travel to the reserve to see elephants trumpeting and hippos bathing in pools of water. Their goal is to create new values in their community, and the Mambas hope that the next generation will grow up wanting to conserve animals, not hunt them.

Africa's animals are still in great danger. In 2017, 1,028 rhinos were poached, an average of three every day. But that number is less than the rhinos killed in 2016—partly thanks to the Black Mambas. With this group of fierce, determined women on their side, Africa's most endangered animals may just have a chance of bouncing back.

The Black Mambas are based in South Africa, home to about 80 percent of the world's rhino population.

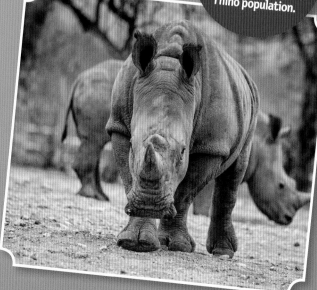

Julia Child

∽ Queen of the Kitchen ∽

"Find something you're passionate about and keep tremendously interested in it."
—*Julia Child*

No one has done more to shape the way we cook and eat food in America than Julia Child. On her TV show *The French Chef*, she was warm, funny, and unafraid to make mistakes on camera. And when she did make mistakes, she didn't get embarrassed. After accidentally flipping a potato pancake out of the skillet and onto the table, she famously looked straight into the camera and declared, "Remember, you are alone in the kitchen and nobody can see you." Her love of food and can-do attitude were infectious, and America fell in love with the French Chef. But many still don't know about her second secret life: as an intelligence officer.

A TASTE FOR ADVENTURE

At six feet two inches (1.9 m), Julia McWilliams was the tallest girl in her class, but she was not one to try to shrink into the background. She was a jokester known for her pranks and was a talented golfer, tennis player, and hunter. When the United States entered World War II, McWilliams wanted to do something to help. She tried to join the Women's Army Corps (WAC) and the United States Naval Reserve (also called the WAVES), but she was turned down for being too tall. So she went to work for the Office of Strategic Services (OSS)—a worldwide spy network that would eventually become the Central Intelligence Agency (CIA).

McWilliams started out as a research assistant typing up note cards. But she rose through the ranks until she was an administrative assistant in charge of organizing a large office. Along the way, she worked as an assistant to scientists trying to develop a shark repellent to protect sailors and airmen who went down in shark-infested waters.

It might have been here that McWilliams found her love of tinkering with recipes: The team experimented with more than 100 different substances, from decayed shark meat to acid, to see if anything would keep the hungry swimmers away. Modern scientists say their winning formula—copper acetate—likely didn't work very well, but at the time, it did a lot to boost the morale of soldiers who were petrified of crash-landing in shark territory.

Julia Child with her husband, Paul (above left), and wielding a mallet on her TV show *The French Chef*, which ran from 1963 to 1973 (above).

BECOMING JULIA

In 1943, McWilliams heard that the OSS was looking for volunteers to serve in Asia. Eager for adventure, she applied and, from 1944 to 1945, she worked in Ceylon (present-day Sri Lanka) and Kunming, China. She served as chief of the OSS registry and had top security clearance. She handled highly classified papers and kept track of every intelligence message that passed through her office. The work was sometimes dangerous—but McWilliams loved the adventure. And while serving in Sri Lanka, she met an OSS officer named Paul Child, the man who would become her husband.

Paul and Julia married in 1946, and two years later, Paul was assigned to work in France. It was there that McWilliams—now Julia Child—fell in love with French cuisine. After spending all her time in the markets and taking cooking classes, she had the idea to bring her passion for French food to America. Along with two collaborators, Simone Beck and Louisette Bertholle, she published a cookbook called *Mastering the Art of French Cooking* in 1961. When she demonstrated how to make an omelet on television during a promotional tour, Child earned so many enthusiastic phone calls and letters that she was offered her own series. It was the beginning of her historic career as America's first celebrity chef. With her passion and fearless attitude, Child inspired a generation of home cooks and forever changed the way Americans saw food.

Royal Rundown

❀ **BORN:** August 15, 1912, Pasadena, California, U.S.A. ❀ **DIED:** August 13, 2004, Montecito, California, U.S.A. ❀ **LED:** American cuisine
❀ **REMEMBERED FOR:** Igniting America's passion for food and sharing it with the world

COMMANDING KINGS

Storyteller and Spy

Roald Dahl (1916–1990)

Julia Child wasn't the only famous person who led a secret double life as a spy. Children's author Roald Dahl, known for such classics as *Matilda*, *The BFG*, and *Charlie and the Chocolate Factory*, also dabbled in espionage. As a young man, the Welsh-born Dahl served as a fighter pilot for Britain's Royal Air Force (RAF) during World War II. In 1940, he was forced to crash-land his plane in the Egyptian desert when he ran out of fuel. Injured but alive, Dahl crawled out of the wreckage—then wrote a story about the experience that launched his writing career. But what the public didn't know is that at the same time that he was beginning to pen some of the most popular books of the 20th century, Dahl was working as an undercover agent for an espionage network called the British Security Coordination, aimed at persuading America to join the war effort.

QUEENS OF CHANGE

Adventure doesn't always mean climbing mountains or traveling to foreign lands. Sometimes, it means being brave enough to step up for what you believe in. The women on these pages became champions of a cause and spent their careers dedicated to righting wrongs they saw in the world. They may not have worn crowns, but we bow to them anyway.

Green Queen:
Wangari Maathai (1940–2011)

Born in Kenya, Wangari Maathai was the first woman in East and Central Africa to earn a doctorate degree, in 1971. But her extraordinary career was just beginning. At the time, Kenya's forests were being devastated as trees were cut down to make way for buildings. Maathai thought that if she could gather women together to plant trees across Kenya, she could help fight deforestation and create jobs for women at the same time. Not everyone was a fan of Maathai's Green Belt Movement: She was tear-gassed by police and thrown in jail for leading protests. But her organization, founded in 1977, grew into one of the largest grassroots movements in Africa, gathering nearly 900,000 women to plant more than 30 million trees. In 2004, Maathai was awarded the Nobel Peace Prize for her fight to help the environment.

Princess With a Purpose:
Diana, Princess of Wales (1961–1997)

On January 15, 1997, the world's most famous princess stepped onto an active minefield in Angola, on the western coast of Africa. Then, with the help of an expert, she detonated a mine in front of reporters from around the world. With that brave act, she drew the public's attention to a tragedy: the millions of land mines that lurked beneath the countryside in war-torn areas, causing horrific injuries to the local people. Diana, Princess of Wales, used her fame to bring attention to causes she believed in, including animal welfare, homelessness, and addiction, but her fight to ban land mines was her biggest crusade. Though she tragically died in a car crash the same year as her trip to Angola, the United Kingdom soon after ratified an international convention banning land mines.

Symbol of Strength:
Helen Keller (1880–1968)

When she was young, Helen Keller was struck with an unknown illness that left her deaf and blind. Curious and intelligent, Keller tried to understand the world around her through touch, smell, and taste. But when she realized that everyone else was communicating with speech—and that she couldn't participate—she became angry. Her family lived in fear of the temper tantrums she threw out of frustration. Many relatives believed Keller should be put in an institution. But everything changed when Keller's parents found her a teacher named Anne Sullivan. With Sullivan's guidance, Keller learned to use sign language, read braille, and even speak. She graduated with honors from Radcliffe College in 1904, then went on to write books and lecture on behalf of people living with disabilities. She was also an enthusiastic political activist, and in 1920, she helped found the American Civil Liberties Union, or ACLU.

Comedian and Icon:
Ellen DeGeneres (1958–)

Gawky, funny, and just plain likable, Ellen DeGeneres is one of America's most beloved comedians. After working as a waitress, house painter, legal secretary, and vacuum saleswoman, she hit it big as a stand-up comedian. Starting in 1986, she began appearing on all the biggest talk shows, including *The Tonight Show* and *The Late Show*, then scored her own prime-time sitcom, *Ellen*, in 1994. In 1997, DeGeneres decided to come out as gay on her show and in real life. She faced intense criticism for showing her true self to the world: Sponsors even pulled their advertising. But human rights activists applauded her, she won an Emmy Award for the episode, and *Time* magazine put her on the cover. A 2015 poll showed that DeGeneres—who began hosting a popular, Emmy-winning daytime talk show in 2003—has influenced how Americans think about gay rights more than any other celebrity in history.

COMMANDING KINGS

Noble Nobel Winner
Kofi Annan (1938–2018)

Few people did as much for the global community as Kofi Annan, a two-term secretary-general of the United Nations. Born in Ghana, Annan studied science, economics, and international affairs. He combined all his passions when he began working for the World Health Organization in 1962; he later went on to specialize in providing health care for refugees displaced by war. Annan led 70,000 United Nations civilian and military peacekeepers in the mid-1990s before becoming the UN chief officer: the secretary-general. In that role, Annan oversaw dozens of peace projects all over the world, from Iraq to East Timor. On the side, he found time to help the UN raise $1.5 billion for the Global AIDS and Health Fund. Annan was honored with the Nobel Peace Prize in 2001.

Hedy Lamarr

∾ Actress by Day, Inventor by Night ∾

Hedy Lamarr was once called "the most beautiful woman in the world." She charmed audiences around the globe as one of the most famous actresses of the 20th century. But Lamarr hated being defined by her looks. After returning from the set at night, she would wash off her movie makeup and begin her secret second job: as an inventor.

From a room in her house transformed into a workshop, Lamarr churned out all kinds of clever creations. She came up with a device that helped people with limited mobility get in and out of the bathtub. She invented a fluorescent dog collar to help keep people's pooches safe at night. She came up with a tablet that, when dropped into a glass of water, would turn the water into soda.

But Lamarr's most important invention was in the field of communications. In the 1940s, Lamarr was glued to the news as World War II unfolded. When German submarines began bombing passenger ships with torpedoes, she felt that she had to help. Lamarr believed that American submarines would have the advantage if they could use radios to control their torpedoes—which were powerful weapons but often didn't hit their targets. She invented a way to make the radio signal hop from frequency to frequency, so that listening enemies couldn't track the signal and jam it. This invention, called spread-spectrum radio, went on to be used in the development of sonar to detect submarines in the water. It was also a vital step in the creation of most of the wireless communication technologies we use today, from Bluetooth to GPS to cell phone networks.

> "Hope and curiosity about the future seemed better than guarantees. The unknown was always so attractive to me ... and still is."
> —Hedy Lamarr

Royal Rundown

❀ **BORN:** November 9, 1914, Vienna, Austria ❀ **DIED:** January 19, 2000, Altamonte Springs, Florida, U.S.A. ❀ **LED:** The silver screen and communications technology
❀ **REMEMBERED FOR:** Advances in the field of wireless communications

Virginia Apgar

❧ Medical Marvel ❧

Y ou may have never heard her name, but Virginia Apgar was probably one of the first people who touched your life. She was the inventor of the Apgar score, a system used across the world for evaluating the health of newborn babies. Smart, tough, and talented, Virginia Apgar was a pioneer of pediatric medicine.

Apgar knew firsthand the tragedy that illness could bring to a family: One of her brothers died before she was born, and the other struggled with childhood illness. By the time she graduated from high school, Apgar was set on being a doctor. But the road ahead was tough: Many medical schools did not allow women, and those who made it through were not given the same opportunities as their male colleagues. In 1933, Apgar graduated fourth in her class from Columbia University's College of Physicians and Surgeons, intent on becoming a surgeon. But the male chair of surgery instead pushed her into anesthesiology—an unrecognized field at the time.

Apgar succeeded anyway. She became an anesthesiologist and director of the department at Columbia—the first woman to become a full professor there. At that time, the number of newborns that died soon after they were born remained high, even though more women were giving birth in hospitals than ever before. Apgar wanted to change that. In 1952, she invented a simple five-point system to quickly assess the condition of a newborn; her method—called the Apgar score—was credited with steadily increasing infant survival rates worldwide. When asked why she never found time to marry during her tireless crusade to improve infant survival, Apgar quipped, "It's just that I haven't found a man who can cook."

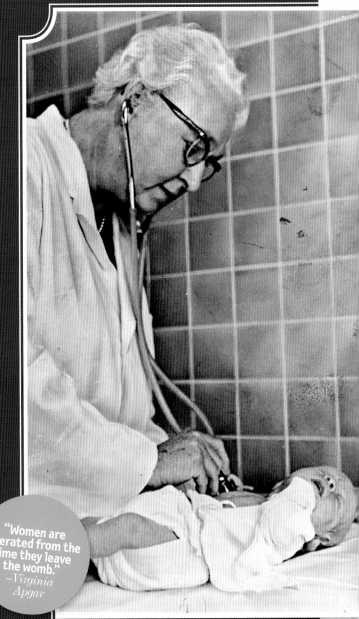

"Women are liberated from the time they leave the womb."
—*Virginia Apgar*

Royal Rundown

❀ **BORN:** June 7, 1909, Westfield, New Jersey, U.S.A. ❀ **DIED:** August 7, 1974, New York, New York, U.S.A. ❀ **LED:** Newborn medical care
❀ **REMEMBERED FOR:** The revolutionary Apgar score for newborns

From climbing the world's tallest peaks to kayaking through dangerous waters to studying lions up close, these trailblazing National Geographic explorers are the reigning royalty of extreme exploration, undertaking grand adventures in every corner of the globe.

Mirna Valerio

Mirna Valerio is an ultramarathon runner, author, and educator who scrambles up mountains on her trail runs and has crossed the finish line in a 62-mile (100-km) mega-marathon. At 250 pounds (113 kg), many people don't believe she looks like a "traditional" runner, and they doubt her athletic abilities, but she is proud of her body and accomplishments. "Fit comes in many forms," Valerio has said. She is determined to inspire other women of all different backgrounds and body types to participate in athletics.

Martina Capriotti

When Martina Capriotti first started scuba diving off Italy's Adriatic coast, she was surprised to see fish feeding around pollution sites. As a way to preserve the beauty and environmental health of her home, she became a marine molecular biologist, a job that requires both serious skills in the laboratory and an adventurous spirit to snorkel and scuba dive to further explore the ocean. She is leading the scientific charge in Italy to test the chemical impact microplastics have on marine animals and their environment.

Freya Hoffmeister

Famed sea kayaker Freya Hoffmeister was the first person to circumvent South America by kayak. During her four-year, 16,700-mile (26,876-km) solo ocean adventure, she paddled through intense winds up to 69 miles an hour (111 km/h), terrifying storms, steep waves, an emergency crash-landing on a rocky coast, and even a broken boat. Hoffmeister's next adventure is an 8-to-10-year journey around North America.

Afghan Women's Cycling Team

In a country where many women are discouraged from competing in sports, they have been shunned, yelled at, and run off the road while trying to practice. But the Afghan Women's Cycling team never stops moving forward. "This is about inspiring the next generation of girls in Afghanistan to follow their dreams, fight for equality, and gain independent mobility," said 2013 National Geographic Adventurer of the Year Shannon Galpin, who volunteered as a coach back in 2012. This determined group of women has successfully competed in bicycling competitions in more than 30 countries and is the subject of a 2018 documentary, *Afghan Cycles*.

Thandiwe Mweetwa

Thandiwe Mweetwa is on a mission to save big cats. She stealthily tracks lions across the savanna in Zambia, where she examines the impact that human encroachment, hunting, and prey depletion have on lion populations. As a child, Mweetwa was inspired by conservation clubs she participated in; now, she trains locals to be conservationists, giving them the same opportunity to be wildlife heroes.

Pasang Lhamu Sherpa Akita

Pasang Lhamu Sherpa Akita triumphantly scaled Mount Everest and K2 (the world's tallest peaks) and became Nepal's first female mountaineering instructor. But she became a hero on multiple fronts when she helped save lives during a devastating earthquake in 2016 and delivered more than 11,000 blankets to survivors. Akita also began a foundation to bring basic education to Nepali communities in need, especially targeted at women and children.

Erin Christine Pettit

Glaciologist and climate change scientist Erin Christine Pettit treks across snow and ice and kayaks through freezing waters from the North Slope of Alaska to Antarctica to study glacial ice temperatures and movements. Because it's so dangerous to get close to crumbling glaciers, Pettit uses underwater microphones to listen to the crashing ice, with the hope that it will help scientists understand what's happening and how it impacts the ocean environment and marine mammal behavior. When she's not investigating ice shelves, Pettit runs Girls on Ice, a week-long program that trains high-school-age girls as scientists.

Your Turn to Wear the Crown

Wangari Maathai,
page 162

Has reading this book about history's mightiest queens made you aspire to sit upon the throne yourself? These days, kingdoms are few and far between. But that doesn't mean you have to give up your royal dreams. Modern-day queens found their own companies, invent new technologies, and take charge of changes they want to see become reality. Nowadays, you don't have to have royal blood—or wait around for a handsome prince—to rule.

Being a great leader is a tough task. The most impressive sovereigns from history ruled with grace and wisdom. They listened to the problems of their people, treated everyone with respect, and strove to be model citizens themselves. They were brave on the battlefield—whether that meant fighting off invaders or battling for human rights. They weren't afraid to take charge, even when the odds were against them. And they never let their heads get too big for their crowns.

Most future leaders won't rule from a castle and command a legion of knights. But there are lessons they can learn from the great queens of the past. Here are a few queenly qualities shared by history's most celebrated rulers.

Queen Victoria,
page 13

Oprah Winfrey,
page 75

1. Queens lead with integrity.

The best queens don't just ask their subjects to do what is right: They are role models their people can look up to.

Tawakkol Karman,
page 65

3. Queens respect the role.

Power can be a tool, or it can be a weapon: It all depends on the person who wields it. The greatest queens are careful to command with tolerance and a strong sense of justice.

2. Queens command with courage.

Some of history's greatest queens were afraid to take the throne. But true leaders must act with confidence to earn the trust of their people.

4. Queens are passionate.

The greatest queens don't just steer the ship: They support the arts and foster their nations' brightest minds. These queens with a cause are the ones we remember best.

5. Queens empower their people.

Above all, great queens never forget that it's the subjects who make the kingdom. Have an open mind, listen to new ideas, and aid innovation. Your power comes from the people you lead.

Sonia Sotomayor,
page 63

Kathryn Sullivan,
page 142

So keep a good grip on your crown and scepter.

With sovereign smarts, a noble sense of justice, and a royal wish to make the world a better place, you too can become a leader whose tale will go down in history.

INDEX

Boldface indicates illustrations.

FOR BRITT, QUEEN OF DREAMING BIG —S.W.D.

Published by National Geographic Partners, LLC. All rights reserved. Reproduction of the whole
or any part of the contents without written permission from the publisher is prohibited.

Since 1888, the National Geographic Society has funded more than 12,000 research, exploration,
and preservation projects around the world. The Society receives funds from National Geographic Partners, LLC,
funded in part by your purchase. A portion of the proceeds from this book supports this vital work.
To learn more, visit natgeo.com/info.

NATIONAL GEOGRAPHIC and Yellow Border Design are trademarks of
the National Geographic Society, used under license.

For more information, visit nationalgeographic.com,
call 1-877-873-6846, or write to the following address:
National Geographic Partners
1145 17th Street N.W.
Washington, D.C. 20036-4688 U.S.A.

Visit us online at nationalgeographic.com/books

For librarians and teachers: ngchildrensbooks.org

More for kids from National Geographic: natgeokids.com

National Geographic Kids magazine inspires children to explore their world with fun yet educational articles
on animals, science, nature, and more. Using fresh storytelling and amazing photography,
Nat Geo Kids shows kids ages 6 to 14 the fascinating truth about the world—
and why they should care. **kids.nationalgeographic.com/subscribe**

For information about special discounts for bulk purchases,
please contact National Geographic Books Special Sales: specialsales@natgeo.com

For rights or permissions inquiries,
please contact National Geographic Books Subsidiary Rights: bookrights@natgeo.com

Designed by Nicole Lazarus, Design Superette

The publisher would like to thank the following people for making this book possible: Kate Hale,
executive editor; Kathryn Robbins, art director; Lori Epstein, director of photography; Jen Agresta,
project editor; Nicole DiMella, photo editor; Lorna Notsch, fact-checker; Ariane Szu-Tu, editor; Alix Inchausti,
production editor; and Anne LeongSon and Gus Tello, production assistants.

Special thanks also to Adrienne Mayor, research scholar,
Classics and History and Philosophy of Science at Stanford University; Laura Miller, Ph.D., Eiichi Shibusawa-Seigo
Arai Endowed Professor of Japanese Studies and professor of history at University of Missouri–St. Louis; and
Jennifer Houser Wegner, associate curator, University of Pennsylvania Museum of Archaeology and Anthropology;
and Dr. Herman Viola.

Hardcover ISBN: 978-1-4263-3535-8
Reinforced library binding ISBN: 978-1-4263-3536-5

Printed in China
19/PPS/1